EUBIE BLAKE
Keys of Memory

Lawrence T. Carter

BALAMP PUBLISHING

DETROIT, MICHIGAN

Library of Congress Cataloging in Publication Data
Carter, Lawrence T
   Eubie Blake.

   Includes index.
      1. Blake, Eubie, 1883-   2. Jazz musicians-
   -United States—Biography.
   ML410.B6247C4   785.4'2'0924 [B]
   ISBN 0-913642-10-X

ISBN 0-913642-10-X
Library of Congress Catalogue No.: LC 79-12430
Copyright © 1979 by Balamp Publishing. All rights reserved.
Printed in the United States of America
10 9 8 7 6 5 4 3 2 1

Balamp Publishing
7430 Second Blvd.
Detroit, Mich. 48202

DEDICATED TO
Chuck Muer, Percy Gabriel
and
Jim Taylor
for their sponsorship, performance
and promotion of
The Best In Ragtime And Jazz

James Hubert ("Eubie") Blake is a part of an original American Musical thing called ragtime. This unique musical form sprang from the soul and native genius of black Americans at a time when they were at their lowest state since their experience of chattel slavery.

During the period of so-called Reconstruction directly after the North-South political deal, all of their effective political and moral safeguards were gone. The rights of the newly-freed blacks were now a mockery. Cut off from the franchise they had so recently enjoyed, barred from any seat of representative or elective power, they were the objects of genocidal thoughts and plans in the calculations of some white leaders of both the North and the South. They faced a perilous situation. Nor was there a Moses to bring the laws and the tablets to them. The wilderness was everywhere about them, and no man could say for sure which way lay the path to the promised land. For in 1864, President Lincoln's American Freedman's Inquiry Commission, which was headed by Robert Dale Owen, reported, "The Negro is genial, lively, docile, and emotional. The affections rule. Cheerfulness and love of mirth overflow with the exuberance of childhood."

Charles Eliot Norton favored a containment of the black man in the South. And these were the thoughts and words of one of the black man's "friends." James Shepherd Pike, no friend of the blacks, advised, "Coop him up, slough him off, preserve just so much of North America as is possible to the white man." Samuel Gridley Howe said, "The race's 'womanly qualities' doom the black man to extinction anyway as a free competitor with the white man." These harsh dicta, the genocidal pattern of these thoughts, probably represented one anti-black extreme. Yet they colored the condition of life for a confused, powerless race.

But the black American was not destined for such a fate.

1

Nor did the open invitation to the process of neglect, starvation and containment prevail. For both blacks and whites, the awareness of each other, the fondness for each other, the mingling of blood, and the actual need for each other under the conditions of existence in America has been and still remains one of the great unsolved puzzles of human life on this planet. The full story of this experience can never adequately be revealed. Deeply hidden in the dark womb of time, the truth lies yet unborn, undefined and forever a human mystery. Some of the marginalia of the story, however, may be examined in the life and works of a black American such as Eubie Blake.

During the past decade, we have heard much about the genetic endowments of the races and the transmission of certain superior or inferior genes. One of these superior qualities, if any do exist, must surely be the ability to survive hardship and deprivation in a hostile environment.

What were the means of black survival? Speculatively, we could adduce various answers and interpretations. It often seems that each American white is some sort of self-contained authority on blacks. Despite disastrous proof that this is not so, the concept nevertheless remains a "truth" in the folkways and personal psychology of American whites. Perhaps there is a need for this belief. In the context of the natural majority-minority situation, the feeling of possessing superior knowledge may serve a useful purpose. Who really knows? The surveys, probings, examinations, measurements and studies by white sociologists, academics and other "experts" fill an enormous niche in the archives of our land. The residual effect of much of this activity has been the amassing and compiling of a great deal of trivial, misleading, even mystifying material. Yet blacks still remain elusive, somewhat of a psychic as well as a social enigma even to themselves.

Since the beginning of the new black consciousness, the black power thrust, national black political caucuses and such related activity, black studies programs have become the new thing on college campuses throughout America. Indeed, understanding blacks has well nigh become a separate and thriving industry.

A vast effort toward identification with "Mother Africa" began on the part of black Americans in the decade of the 1960s. Today, concerts of Afro-American music and dance and black drama workshops and experimental theaters proliferate in all of our major cities. The works of black playwrights and poets are produced and acclaimed on Broadway and in the citadels of our intellectual elite. This new black pride and awareness indicates, in its entirety, a startling new American phenomenon.

Hollywood has discovered black gold. The great American dream factory has fashioned a new black identity machine. Once only marginally profitable, movie palaces located in the downtowns of many partly-decayed American cities have now become "black houses." Emergent black script writers, directors, actors and entrepreneurs are busy confecting and purveying this new blackness. All of the special talents, insights and commercial abilities of this burgeoning industry are cleverly utilized to produce these "exploitation films" by and for blacks. With a few notable exceptions, the end result of this trend is to create an image of lust, lawlessness and a special kind of black depravity. While this presents a cruel, debased picture of black Americans, it somehow fills a need and is therefore profitable. It must surely reinforce the idea of the whites who control and ultimately garner the major financial returns from these films that they, in truth, really do know what blacks need and want.

Slowly, quietly, however, in the emergent awareness of black creativity, there has also been a solid and growing interest in ragtime. This great musical form, the mother lode of rhythmic and melodic invention produced in America, is now enjoying a national interest and appreciation. But oddly enough, the prime

3

movers and supporters of this renaissance have been whites. In 1950, Rudi Blesh and Harriett Janis published their landmark book, *They All Played Ragtime.* This work presented a great mine of information as the authors, through their patient and painstaking research, revealed much about the mysterious genesis and development of this great musical form in the hearts, minds and fingers of black America. *They All Played Ragtime* seems somehow to bear a mystical resemblance to W.E.B. DuBois' *Souls of Black Folk.* There are echoes of the hardship, the bafflement, and the poignancy of black joy and frustration in both works. Yet out of this wilderness of black confusion came an affirmation of happiness, measure and order. It was expressed in the capture and the codification of the rhythms and counterrhythms and the melodies and countermelodies of a complex and beautiful structural order. This seedbed of melody, rhythm and pure joyous invention was the base from which America's one real original cultural creation has grown.

I is surely not difficult to trace the lineal musical descent of all of the forms of jazz, gospel and rock in existence today to these humble beginnings in the dark bayous and backwaters of ragtime.

Despite the black provenance of ragtime, however, one notices that in the acknowledgments contained in the third and revised edition of *They All Played Ragtime,* only three blacks are mentioned. They are Billy Taylor, Hank Jones and Jaki Byard. Of course, it is natural that out of any art form will evolve many variations and changes. Otherwise, art would be static. No closed circle of practice or taste can prevent each succeeding generation of artists, in whatever medium, from carrying the art form to a different, if not always higher, level of development. And the demand by the purveyors of popular culture and entertainment create an ever-changing atmosphere of the new, the sensational, and ofttimes merely the bizarre. This, in sum,

4

is what has happened to ragtime in the lifetime of one of America's originals—Eubie Blake.

When Eubie relates the incidents surrounding the creation of "Shuffle Along," the great Broadway musical of 1922, he says, "I could write like the white Broadway composers, Jerry Kern and fellows like that [if I wanted to]." Inferentially, he means that the demands of the white theatrical world dictated that a black composer must bend to the winds of change in order to stay abreast of the current popular musical demand. And thereby hangs a tale.

Let us consider an article in *Downbeat* magazine, April 1, 1971, by Paul R. Lentz. The author is writing about trumpeter Wallace Davenport. He opens thus: "Does it not seem paradoxical that black people in great numbers shun Dixieland jazz? In some circles, mention of any Dixieland-oriented group brings the response, 'Man, that's Uncle Tom music!' This virile music has often been castrated by a collection of clowns, hacks and musical bunco artists who chose the least desirable elements of the genre." How true! But is that all? Is that really the whole story? To answer these questions, one must recognize two facts. Number one is the effort among blacks to put away any semblance or memory of their inferior status. The rejection of ragtime and Dixieland represents a harsh black rejection of the American stereotype which blacks have come to hate—that of a happy, carefree, shuffling, eyerolling creature of low comedy and campy cuteness. Number two is the bending of the black creative will to the everchanging demands of the white entertainment establishment. To a great extent, these two ideas point out the unique situation of the black man in a white world—that of an entertainer. His speech, his dress, his lifestyle, his music, even his rage and protest at the basic situation of the inferior status he faces in our land is, to a great extent, pure entertainment to white Americans. He remains something apart.

His fury, his rebellion, his often bitter frenzy and violence is a regular source of material to be presented by T.V. and the other media for the amusement of whites.

Black consciousness, black pride and the urge to identify completely with "Mother Africa" all represent a vast, almost pietistic, effort of a people to discover and bring back a lost past. We have witnessed a joyous but serious effort to restructure a modern bond of continuity with an African past clouded in forgotten black glories and partly mythic empires of power and high cultural achievement. Yet at the same time, in America, blacks are now rejecting a present-day black cultural achievement of the first order—ragtime. A modest part of the moneys and effort spent on black studies might well have resurrected and enshrined the real true greatness of this original American cultural contribution. Sadly enough, this represents a basic white-induced shame on the part of American blacks to accept what is perhaps the greatest contribution of their American past. The hardships, struggle and brutal exploitation of the Poles by other nations and peoples is one of the ethnic tragedies of the past few centuries. Yet can one imagine a child of Polish blood anywhere on earth who does not know of and venerate Chopin? Therefore, in the same context of cultural and racial pride, why should not every black American child know and venerate Scott Joplin and Eubie Blake?

In January, 1972, Atlanta's Morehouse College conducted a week-long seminar on black culture. Scott Juplin's black opera "Treemonisha" was presented in its premiere performance at Constitution Hall in Atlanta. It was a great occasion. The event marked the culmination of a week of seminars and discussion by many famous participants. Eubie Blake was escorted as a guest of honor to the front of the auditorium and seated directly behind the conductor of the Atlanta Symphony Orchestra, which furnished the musical accompaniment for the opera. The veneration accorded Blake at this premiere and at the gala reception which was held later gave evidence that black cultural achievement was at last being given its rightful due by blacks. Yet the entire affair was made possible by white money in the form of a grant from the Ford Foundation. And the opera was partly orchestrated and produced through great efforts of William Bolcom, a white ragtime interpreter and enthusiast, and Vera Brodsky Lawrence, who had done years of patient research into partly-lost and forgotten Scott Joplin musical compositions.

And so it has been for many years. Various white ragtime organizations have kept alive this black musical idiom. Rudi Blesh, the late Harriett Janis, the Ragtime Society of Toronto, Ragtime Bob Darch, Max Morath, Russ Cassidy, Trebor Tichenor and Mike Montgomery have all constituted an international network of ragtime enthusiasts, connoisseurs and preservers of the past glories of this music.

Nostalgia, like love, is difficult to define. There is a vague feeling of something lost, something gone which is associated with a past happiness. Its shape is a congruence of unstated and ineffable feelings of longing. The sounds of delight and the echoes of spent laughter, happy voices and carefree times are conjured out of the depths of memory. This forgotten garden of dreams can ofttimes be re-entered and rediscovered through the sounds of the music of the past. But nostalgia is a state of elusive charm. It is perhaps the opposite of regret.

Nostalgia appears then, in opposition to regret, as something pleasant, even desirable. Can it be that white America has resurrected and worked to sustain ragtime as an instinctive prompter of the memory of a former time when America was simpler and less troubled? When the dollar was sound, the "certainties" of life unquestioned and the blacks "knew their place" and kept it? Conversely, can it be that black regret at the loss and hardship since emancipation makes ragtime to

7

them a memory of a crisis of the black soul and thus something to be shut away and buried in a regretted past? If this be true, then it is one of the greatest cultural tragedies which the race has sustained. To reject a splendid past cultural contribution out of shame, fear and anger is to lose a precious link in racial tradition.

CHAPTER 2

The life of Eubie Blake is a testimony to the wonder and greatness of America. Born on February 7, 1883, in Baltimore, Maryland, the city where Frederick Douglass, as a slave and apprentice caulker, learned to read and write, he entered life at a time which seems now to be clouded in the mist of forgetfulness and legend. The mighty effort of America to achieve her true potential of greatness had just seriously begun.

U.S. Grant was then President of the United States. The vast smoky haze of the Appalachians, the rich fields of the newly-bestirred South and the great fertile plains of the West cried out for the hand, the pick and the plow. Coal, cotton, wheat, steel, oil and gold lay fallow in rich abundance. They awaited the energy of man to release them. Ribbons of steel rails traced the rights-of-way of the new railroad empires which had begun to probe the Western frontier. Great swelling inland rivers carried ever more bountiful and diverse cargoes of goods and traders to and fro in these regions. The inland ports along these streams rang out with the shouts and the clamor of the brawny enthusiasm of a burgeoning class of American travelers and traders. It was a tumultuous, exciting time for adventure and enrichment. There was the thrill of a newly-opened land to be mastered and tamed. The American dream was producing a new episode of wonder and delight. Savage unbridled energies were to be released to make this dream come true.

Amidst this torrential flow of goods and commodities there was a place for the black man. He pulled the barges and toted the bales. On the riverboats were the roustabouts who traveled endlessly up and down, to and fro, between the citadels of this new and growing commerce. Like Flaubert's mercenaries at Carthage, they worked and sometimes played, leading the lives of strong, unreflective animals. Reckless, rootless, they lived and died while America literally burst at the seams with commercial and industrial expansion. And in the port cities and rivertrading towns, the more settled blacks with established families became the stevedores. Throughout this period, the great new inland trading region was infused with a frontier energy that bordered upon savagery. Here the effete East held no cultural sway whatsoever. The work, the play, in fact the very quality of everyday existence bore quite cruel and savage overtones. But this was not a savagery of hate born of the memories of religious repression or ethnic rivalries. Rather it was the savagery of untrammeled freedom and animality. The cruel winters with their great snows, the howling winds and the sun-baked prairies as well as the tumultuous flooding freshets of spring were a challenge to man, not only for survival but also for mastery, and his response was equal to the challenge.

Without the amenities of a more settled existence, the crudity of natural emotions held sway. Relaxation was often as strenuous as work. Bearbaiting and coonbaiting, cockfighting, brawling, boozing and whoring where possible were the pleasures of the day. In this atmosphere, where blacks were chiefly the menials, they also gradually became the entertainers.

The plunk of the banjo and the wail of the mouth-harp were often heard from belowdecks on the riverboats. The flickering light of the oil lamp would reveal a circle of black figures engaged in a riotous, happy hoedown while whites, on the decks above, would watch, laughing and swaying and stomping in time to these crude melodies and dances.

Gradually, though, along with the establishment of the new river trading towns came new comforts and amenities. And the finest, gaudiest, most ornate and most comfortable of these new amenities were to be found in the whorehouses. Here, black performers, chiefly piano men, were the staple of entertainment.

A tradition had been born which, at the time of Eubie Blake's birth in 1883, was already thriving.

Itinerant black piano plunkers had begun to trade, embellish and codify the swelling African music which they felt within themselves. Intricate rhythmical patterns were developed. Abrupt chord changes as well as long beautiful melodic lines became the *lingua musica* of this band of black troubadors who lived in and traveled among the Southern and mid-American river towns. The white folks made money; the black folks made music. Thus it was in the Baltimore of Eubie's childhood.

CHAPTER 3

It is difficult for the youth of today to cross the generation gap. It is also as difficult for the average American of whatever age to understand the condition of the black masses in America in 1883, the year of Eubie's birth. Their survival and advancement is a saga of hope, tenacity, religion, grudgingly-paid-for labor and song. In 1874, on July 28, only nine years before Eubie was born, the Freedman's Savings Bank closed with nearly three million dollars owing to black depositors. Founded in 1865 for the purpose of helping the freed slaves in their new environment, it had before long developed thirty-four branches, extending from New Orleans to Philadelphia, and the money of the ex-slaves flowed into its coffers. Growing rich, it built a tremendous and gaudy central office in Washington, D.C. But then, with practically nothing in ready assets, it collapsed, mainly because of the dishonesty of some of its officials. There were several rather half-hearted efforts to have the federal government make good the loss, since it had taken a direct interest in the enterprise, but these efforts came to nothing. There then existed no Federal Deposit Insurance Corporation, so the depositors were simply out of luck.

In the Baltimore of Eubie's birth, there were mills and factories which manufactured saddlery and harness tanners' products, all kinds of printed matter, tinware, paper boxes, soap, engines and machinery, chrome, roofing paper, beer, whiskey, type and stencils, burglar-proof safes, bottles and glassware, millinery, oils, drugs, chemicals, patent medicines, fertilizer and many other products.

In October of 1889, the first pig iron for the manufacturing of Bessemer steel was cast at Furnace A at Sparrows Point, Maryland, not far from Baltimore. On August 1, 1891, the first Bessemer steel made in Maryland was blown and rolled into rails. Earlier, in 1890, the construction of the shipyard had begun. In 1892, its first product, the tugboat Penwood, was launched. There followed passenger and freight steamers for Chesapeake Bay service and the steamer Glouchester for the Boston line of the Merchants and Miners Transportation Company. Rails were shipped from Sparrows Point to England, Scotland, Ireland, Italy, South Africa, India, China, Japan, Australia, Siberia, Norway and Sweden. In 1893, Sparrows Point had the only hydraulic shears capable of lifting one-hundred-and-fifty-tons and was the only one on the seaboard capable of hoisting from the steamer the one-hundred-and-twenty-five-ton gun which was shipped from Germany by Krupp to the Columbian Exposition.

This great industrial complex had drawn black labor from the neighboring states and from the deep South. These men sweated and ate the smoke and grime of its blast furnaces, molding sheds and shops, and lived womanless in its shanties and shacks. Their payday forays into the businesses, dives and sporting houses of Baltimore fed its meager black economy as well as that of the whites.

The Baltimore docks also employed many blacks as stevedores. Eubie's father was one, ill-paid and with the usual ups and downs of employment. When he was unemployed, the family sustained itself on the magnificent sum of ninety dollars every three months, which John Blake received as his Civil War service pension. To supplement that, Emily Blake washed and cleaned for the white folks. "Peabody Institute, did I study music there?" laughs Eubie. "The only memory I have of Peabody Institute is of white kids from Peabody pushing me off the sidewalks when I was delivering washing for my mother in the white neighborhoods.

Great Baltimore—seaport, manufacturing giant, home of

Johns Hopkins University, Peabody Institute, Baltimore Museum of Art, and the Enoch Pratt Free Library, which as late as 1959 had no mention of Joe Gans in its index. This same Gans, childhood friend of Eubie Blake, was, by accepted opinion, one of the great sons of Baltimore, lightweight boxing champion of the world and surely one of the greatest pugilists who ever lived. Today, a grocery store occupies the building at Lexington and Colvin Streets which once housed his famous Goldfield Hotel. Thus often runs the course of black fame and remembrance in America.

CHAPTER 4

Today, Eubie Blake resides in Brooklyn on Stuyvesant Avenue, a street which is, like much of Brooklyn, one continuous wall of aging brownstones. Across the street, on the corner of Stuyvesant and Bridge Streets, stands the massive structure of the Bridge Street A.M.E. Church. Constantly busy during the daylight hours, it is the center of various neighborhood activities, and sometimes as many as four funerals a day are held here. Watching from Eubie's windows, one sees a funeral party pull up to the curb. At the same time, a coffin is carried out of the building, and a group of mourners walks slowly down the worn yellowed stone steps, enters waiting automobiles, and drives away. Now it is the newly-arrived mourners' turn to enter. The last rites of yet another departed citizen are about to begin.

The ground floor door of Eubie's house, which once belonged to his wife Marion's family, is covered by a massive sheet of steel. This accommodates both an inside lock of immense proportions and a convenient peephole for the identification of the caller. It is a precaution, Mrs. Blake tells you, made necessary because of the high incidence of burglaries and break-ins in the neighborhood. The back windows of the house are also securely barred. The back door of the ground floor opens upon a rather ample enclosed back yard. Here, in summer, vines climb the mellowed brick walls on three sides while flowers, mostly shade-loving varieties, show their heads at various intervals beneath these walls. In the center of the court stands a large outdoor table, around which are placed four or five metal chairs. But although this courtyard exhibits all of the possibilities for open-air living and entertaining, it is seldom put to actual use. Inside, the rooms are comfortably air-conditioned, and the noises from the street and the surrounding neighbor-

15

hood make indoor living highly preferable, even in summer.

Eubie doesn't mind. He is essentially a night person; habits of more than sixty years have become a part of his life. "I can't go to sleep until three or four o'clock, because my system won't let me," says Eubie. "I've been staying up all night for so long that I just can't change now." He doesn't mind, he explains, although it does get lonesome at times. To keep himself busy until he gets sleepy, he generally works on "something musical," such as composing or arranging. He also enjoys going out at night to parties or to Manhattan night spots with Carl Seltzer, a young man whom Marion and Eubie call their "white child."

Carl is a theatrical lighting technician who hopes to find steady employment in his trade on Broadway. A dedicated lover of ragtime, he met Eubie long ago at the Village Vanguard during the appearance of one of Eubie's old colleagues, Willie the Lion.

To spend a typical day at the Blake home in Brooklyn is to be rewarded with the company of two lovable people. Although Eubie is a night person, Marion is not, and during the day she is up and about the business of being a housewife-secretary. She is precise, punctual and impressive in her remarkable capacity for detail.

Breakfast with Marion is a leisurely and pleasant experience. Naturally, much of her talk is about Eubie. She speaks fondly of him, and his sleeping habits bother her none whatsoever. "I can get so much accomplished while he is asleep of a morning," she says. "Of course," she adds, "he's never in the way. It's just that I'm used to his habits."

The large three-story brownstone where the Blakes have lived since their marriage is a chore for her now, she says, because she has not been able to find a dependable housekeeper. "Sometimes I feel hopeless about it," she admits. Because of this, at

16

one time they considered moving to a senior citizens' facility in Brooklyn. Carl took them over to be interviewed, and Marion was very much impressed. But Eubie was not, and so, as Marion says, "We came home. We have never discussed it further."

Another chore which is too much for her is the sorting out of Eubie's papers. He has a huge collection of manuscripts, photographs and other mementos of his long career, and Marion feels that something should really be done about preserving them in some orderly fashion. Eubie agrees and has said that he wishes to leave them to Hampton Institute. But it is not as easy as that. Elliott Hoffman, their lawyer, has told them that the arrangements must be made through proper legal means; so far neither Eubie nor Hoffman has gotten around to drawing up the necessary documents.

On the second floor, Marion ushers you into Eubie's bedroom (he is asleep in another room down the hall). Near the window, which overlooks Stuyvesant Avenue, is Eubie's bed. On a stand near the bed is a great slab of plaster, almost three inches thick and about two and a half feet wide by three feet long. "This fell from the ceiling onto the bed months ago," says Marion. "Fortunately, he wasn't in it!" She has been trying unsuccessfully for several months now to get the hole repaired, but so far nothing has been done. She laughs. "[The plaster chunk] . . . is a testimony that God loves Eubie."

The room is filled with musical manuscripts stacked on tables and on the floor and in every imaginable nook and corner. In addition, the walls are covered with photographs of performers whose careers extend from sixty-five years ago to the present. There are piles of sheet music of songs dating back to the beginning of the century, as well as of numerous revues, and over Eubie's desk are old faded pictures of Emily and John Sumner Blake, his parents. The room is so rich in memorabilia that it

17

takes on the quality of a museum.

Also filled with memorabilia is the front hallway, with its photographs of black and white musical and theatrical greats. Here are Bert Williams, Ada Walker, George Walker, Ernest Hogan, Jack Johnson, Noble Sissle with an early mandolin band; Bojangles, Broadway Jones, Lucky Roberts, Willie the Lion, James P. Johnson, Fats Waller, Jim Europe, Josephine Baker, Florence Mills, Lena Horne, Claudia McNeill and many other stars of the present era as well as bye-gone ones.

It is now well past noon but Eubie is still asleep. Marion takes you into their bar, located near the photo gallery. It is small but well-stocked. Near the back door is another small room, this one containing two refrigerators, one with an ample supply of tonic, ice cubes and limes. Sipping a gin and tonic, Marion stands before a photograph of Florence Mills and the chorus line of the Lew Leslie show "Dixie to Broadway," which opened in Long Branch, New Jersey, in 1924 and finally came to a successful run at the Broadhurst Theater in New York. Near the end of the chorus line is Marion herself. She smiles. "I know what you're thinking," she says. "You're asking yourself why I look so sad in that picture." Her first husband, Billy Tyler, made Leslie put her in that chorus line, she explains. A talented violin player, he usually got everything he wanted ("But not the success he deserved," she muses). However, Marion was not a very good dancer. In fact, Leslie thought she was so bad that he even told Billy, "You know, I never heard of a colored woman who couldn't dance!" He couldn't fire her, of course, and Billy didn't want Marion to quit, so she remained in the show. But she was not too happy about it.

Marion continues reminiscing about Billy's career. After "Dixie to Broadway," he performed with Florence Mills' show at the Plantation Theater at Broadway and Fiftieth Street. When he left that show, he went to Chicago with another one called

"Strut Miss Lizzie." Chicago was Billy's home, and they had a wonderful time there. Finally, though, they left Chicago for Detroit.

In Detroit, Billy appeared at E.B. Dudley's Koppin Theater. Dudley booked all of the "colored" acts and shows in those days and he was thrilled to get Billy to conduct and play in his band. He was so thrilled, in fact, that he not only installed the Tylers in his own home and put Marion in the box office, but he even bought them a new automobile (which they refused). As time passed, however, the Tylers noticed an odd thing. They stopped receiving any mail or telegrams. Since they didn't care for Detroit, they were quite disturbed about this. The mystery was cleared up, however, when Marion received a frantic call one day from Will Vodery in New York. "Why haven't you answered my telegrams?", he demanded. "I want Billy to go to Europe with my band for an extended tour." Marion hastened to explain that she and Billy hadn't received them. Obviously Dudley had been so anxious to keep Billy that he had been intercepting his mail. It had worked for a while, but his plan had now been foiled; the Tylers soon left for Europe.

Marion looks sad: "Billy had a fine career, [but] he never really got his big chance. Maybe now he would; times have changed for Negro artists. But poor Billy died, I think, of a broken heart. He got so despondent that for several years he wouldn't touch his violin."

CHAPTER 5

In the Blake house, the afternoon breeze is gentle and caressing through the doors to the sunny courtyard. The kitchen table has been set for breakfast for one. Presently Eubie enters, smiling and sunny in manner, as always. Marion asks if he has slept well. Winking impishly, he replies, "Yeah. I always sleep well once I get started." Marion then goes on to tell him that Dean Martin's office had phoned earlier, wanting him to tape with them in Los Angeles the following month. "Did they talk about the fee?", Eubie questions. "Is the money all right?" She assures him that they were quite generous in their offer. "The papers are in Manhattan," she adds. "You'll have to go over there to sign them."

Eubie's breakfast is his usual light one—a dish of fruit, a doughnut and coffee. As he eats, Marion reminds him that ragtime enthusiasts Rudi and Ada Blesh are coming over later that day. This means that he has to hurry, for today is the day he makes his weekly trip downtown to Schraft's for his supply of doughnuts and candy.

Eubie goes to get dressed. When he returns he presents himself to Marion, waiting for her comments on his outfit. She eyes him for a moment, critical of his tie. But she finally agrees that he looks "fine" in spite of it, and so he leaves the house.

A trip downtown with Eubie on the number Twenty-six bus is a special experience. On the way he regales you with marvelous tales and precious memories of his Brooklyn "adventures." As he talks, the bus rattles past miles of decaying, aging brownstones. It is a depressing panorama. Once inside Schraft's, however, the atmosphere changes. Eubie takes you to his special counter, where a lovely ritual is enacted. Atop the counter is

20

a neat bundle of doughnuts, cookies and hard candies. Eubie's usual saleslady then approaches, mature and pleasant-voiced, an echo of a past day when shopping was gracious and the customer was valued as a person.

"Oh, Mr. Blake," she exclaims, "it's so good to see you again. I have your bundle here; it's all ready for you." Eubie smiles, and as he accepts and pays for his package, they exchange pleasantries.

On the bus homeward Eubie says, "That lady is one of the nicest persons I have ever known. It's strange, but my life has been filled with lovely people like her. I guess I've been blessed." And a look of serenity crosses his face. He then goes on to explain about the sweets. It is because he doesn't drink any alcohol, he says. In fact, he doesn't even eat fruit cake, as it might be flavored with "spirits."

It has been over twenty-five years since he has had a drink. It was not easy to quit, but once he had made up his mind to do it, he would not be deterred. At first he tried substitutes. His initial choice was tea. He almost drove Marion out of her mind, but she is a "dear person" and supported him in his efforts. "I brewed up enough tea to support China," he chuckles. "I had tea in all the pots and pans and kettles in Marion's kitchen!" In spite of all this, unfortunately, it didn't work. The only noticeable effect which those gallons of tea produced on Eubie was that he kept running to the bathroom!

Root beer was his next idea. It was served to him one night at a party in Manhattan and, as Eubie says, "I liked the stuff. I said to myself, 'This is it. This root beer is better than tea.'" So he came home, poured out the tea and started brewing root beer instead. Soon the kitchen was filled with it. But again Marion was patient. And this time it worked. Eubie was through with alcohol for good.

21

Back on Stuyvesant Avenue, Eubie wants to stop and get some green vegetables for Marion. As he walks, his slender figure seems to glide along the sidewalk like a sail in the shifting currents of the summer breeze. Suddenly a protruding piece of sidewalk causes him to stumble, and he sways slightly. Steadied by a gentle grip on his elbow, he smiles gratefully. "It's my legs that are a bit uncertain," he admits. "I was just telling [that to] Ted Lewis the other day. I said, 'Ted, . . . we're both all right, but it's the legs. [They] go first and then we get a little bit wobbly.'" He then asks you to be sure to steady him when he goes into the grocery store. The owner tells everyone that Eubie is a drunkard, he explains. Why else would he be staggering every time he comes into the store? With that, Eubie exploded with a long, loud burst of laughter.

CHAPTER 6

Back home again, Eubie takes a short nap and is then ready for dinner. As you watch him, you realize that although the world has been singing his songs for more than fifty years, he is still strong, alert and full of lively exhuberance.

He is quick to tell you that he is the son of former slaves. "Be sure to note that," he will say. His lifetime partner and friend, Noble Sissle, used to ask him why he mentioned it. As a graduate of Butler University, he somehow felt that one should not bring up such facts anymore. But Eubie is not ashamed. "My parents were proud, decent, God-fearing black people from Virginia," he says, "and they instilled a pride in me that has lasted for a long, active lifetime."

Eubie admits that he has had little formal education. Mathematics was his downfall—he could never understand it. But he has played his compositions on Broadway and in Europe, and has entertained not only royalty but "practically all the millionaires and socialites of New York, Newport, Southampton and Palm Beach." The early family pride which he received from his parents plus a lifetime of song and musical composition have left in him an urbanity and a quiet gentility which are unmistakable.

Stubbing out his ever-present cigarette, "the one remaining vice I can practice," he finishes his rather spare meal. The telephone rings and is brought to the small settee on which he is sitting. A newspaper man is calling. Eubie chats for awhile and then says, "Thanks. Goodbye." No sooner does he hang up than the phone rings again. This time it is his host of the previous evening, inquiring about the late Wilbur Sweatman. He is attempting to locate some of his compositions. "Well, yes, I knew Wilbur well," says Eubie, nodding his head at the phone.

"Great guy, great musician he was. I got his widow lined up with ASCAP . . .; got her some royalties from his works." He thinks that Dick Gregory, the "great comedian from St. Louis," would know all about Sweatman's remaining relatives.

The conversation turns to Scott Joplin. "Yeah, yeah, I knew Scott Joplin slightly," says Eubie. "He was a fine man." He recalls meeting Joplin once at a Washington banquet, in 1906 or 1907. "Maple Leaf Rag" was the composition which made him famous, but Eubie does not consider that to be his greatest achievement. He also wrote an opera called "Treemonishia." "I had the entire books and let it get away from me somehow." Eubie says. "People don't return things; don't ever lend books." He looks stern but then chuckles, relenting in his mind, and goes on relating the story of his meeting with Joplin. A banquet had been given for them in Baltimore, and afterwards they went over to Washington. Contrary to the common belief, Eubie states that there *were* black-owned places even in those days on Pennsylvania Avenue, including a bar and cabaret owned by a woman named Mrs. Brown and another bar owned by a man whose name Eubie cannot remember. It was to one of these clubs that the "Baltimore piano sharks" went that night, and after all of them had played for the crowd, the request went up for Joplin to play also. He was already old then, and those who had known him from around Sedalia, Missouri, told Eubie that he had never been much of a performer. "But he could write," muses Eubie, breaking into the events of his story. "Oh boy, he could write!" Joplin talked quietly to Eubie that night, explaining that he just could not play. And Eubie understood and did not insist. "He had a quality of what you call humility," he says, "and I respected him." Eubie calls Joplin the "Daddy of Ragtime." He says that some people claim that "some white guy" invented ragtime, but he chuckles as he compares the "white folks" to the Russians, "always claiming what

24

they want to claim." But since ragtime was, in those days, considered to be the dirtiest and lowest form of music, the music of the dives and bars and sporting houses, he doubts that it originated with the "white folks" after all.

After dinner and much banter at the table, Eubie relaxes once more on his favorite sofa in the living room. Lighting the inevitable cigarette, he moves the ash tray closer, crosses one of his frail legs and continues with his reminiscing.

"Now I want to tell you about something that I don't remember," he says. "They said it happened, but I don't remember it." When Eubie was about four years old his parents would go down to the market late on Saturday evenings, because the prices were lowered right before closing time. On this particular evening, although little Eubie was supposed to be trailing along behind them, when his mother turned around to look for him he was nowhere in sight. In a panic she began running back up the street, screaming, "My child! Where is my child?" Finally a man approached and told her that he had seen a little boy going across the street to where a man was selling organs. Sure enough, there was Eubie, up on the platform pressing the keys on the organ and trying to make music. However, since he didn't know that he also had to pump the pedals, no sound was coming out. Happy and angry at the same time, his mother rushed up and grabbed him, but just as she was about to spank him the organ salesman intervened. "Don't spank him, Lady," the man pleaded. "The boy is a genius. He ran away to make music. Buy him one of these organs; you'll never regret it." And putting the hard sell on Mrs. Blake, he somehow signed her up to have an organ delivered on the following Monday. The terms were a dollar down and twenty-five cents a week, but even though Eubie's father was out of work at the time and she didn't have the dollar, the organ was still

25

delivered on Monday morning, all shiny and brand new. Eubie's mother was a proud woman. Too embarrassed to tell the man to take the organ away, she managed to scrape up the dollar for him. Years later, after Eubie had become well-known, the organ salesman—Eubie thinks his name was Eisenbrand—claimed that he had paid for Eubie's training. "That's a lie," scoffs Eubie. "He was just trying to get a little cheap publicity."

At first Eubie couldn't play the organ because he was too little. But he found out how it worked, and soon he was taking "pie-ano" lessons from Margaret Marshall, a young woman who lived up the street from the Blakes. It was not very common in those days for an "ordinary" black family to own a piano, but some white people had given it to Margaret's mother years before. Eubie learned fast, and after Margaret had taught him all that she could, he began to take lessons from Lewellen Wilson, a black orchestra leader. Wilson was very interested in the talented youngster and it was he who taught Eubie how to write music without having to sit down at the piano. But Eubie never forgot his debt to Margaret Marshall. Years later, when he was making good money from playing and from tips in Atlantic City, he would visit her whenever he returned to Baltimore and give her some money, sometimes as much as forty or fifty dollars. "You see," explains Eubie. "I always appreciate what people do for me." But it had never taken much urging to get the young boy to practice his piano lessons. "Music just fascinated me," he recalls.

CHAPTER 7

Talking about his childhood makes Eubie think about his father. He looks down at the cigarette he is smoking. "Now I've been smoking cigarettes for about eighty years," he says. "They say they will kill you, but I'm willing to take a chance after eighty years!" Eubie shifts his legs, blows an immense cloud of smoke and chuckles softly, remembering how his habit got started. When he was still in school his mother would give him several pennies each day to buy fish cakes for lunch. Instead, however, at recess Eubie would slip around the corner to Mrs. Edmonds' little store and buy two pennies worth of cigarettes, claiming that they were for his father. (In those days, Eubie explains here, they would break a pack and sell the cigarettes individually.) "Boy," says Eubie, "if John Sumner Blake had ever found that out, he'd have killed me!"

Mr. Blake was actually a gentle man, though, one who "wouldn't hurt a bug even." He always said that a bug's life was just as precious to the bug as a person's life was to him. That "precious life stuff" wore thin, however, when it came to the rats in their neighborhood, "the biggest rats . . . of anyplace in the world." One time the sewer holes on Blakes' street were blocked up, and when their outlet to the street was gone, the rats began coming into the houses. Finally, in desperation, Eubie's father bought a big cage, baited it with cheese and caught a huge rat. Giving Eubie three cents to go out and buy some kerosene, he then doused the rat with it, threw a burning rag into the cage and opened the cage door. The rat leaped out, fur blazing, and scurried down into a hole. "He must have told all the other rats, 'Don't bother around that Blake house,' " chuckles Eubie, " 'cause we were never bothered anymore!"

Eubie's thoughts return to his music and how it influenced

27

his life. One of his earliest friends was a boy named Harold "Hoppy" Johns; he appears in a photo in one of Eubie's albums. Eubie was a small boy, so small that everyone except Hoppy called him "Mouse." He couldn't fight very well, either, so Hoppy did his fighting for him. "Let me have him, Eubie," Hop would say, and would then proceed to beat the other boy up. They were so close that when the Blakes finally moved, the Johnses moved also—right next door.

Besides Hoppy's ability as a fighter, Eubie also admired his friend's musical talents—the boy could play glissandi on the coronet. In the area of music, however, Eubie's small size was no drawback, because he had the long skinny fingers so advantageous to a piano or organ player. They were so long and skinny, in fact, that when he and his mother boarded a streetcar, she would admonish him, "Close your hands. Don't let your fingers hang down. People will think you're a pickpocket!" Eubie laughs at the memory. "It made me feel bad, but she didn't mean any harm."

By the time Eubie was thirteen, his organ playing fame had spread throughout the neighborhood and he had become quite cocky about his ability. But as Eubie puts it, ". . . Don't care how great you think you are, someone will come 'round and top you." His downfall came at a lawn party given by a girl he liked. He was invited, of course, as he was to all the neighborhood parties. After all, he was the only boy who could play the kind of ragtime they wanted to dance to. Also invited, however, was a boy named Edgar Dowell, who came from a section of Baltimore known as Lynchville. Always before, whenever another boy sat down to play the organ, Hop would say, "Go get 'im, Eubie. Wipe 'im out!" And Eubie would. This time, however, things were different. Edgar could really play. Hearing him, Eubie realized at once that, for a change, it was he who would be "wiped out." There was no way that he could compete. And when he looked up he saw that "his girl" had her arm around Edgar's shoulder. It was too much! In shame and misery Eubie sneaked out to the yard and hid behind a big sycamore tree. Soon it came time for him to play, because the youngsters wanted to dance, but he was nowhere to be found. Finally Hop located him behind the tree, crying as if his heart would break, because he had not only been "wiped out" but had also lost his girl. "Oh, this was a beautiful girl," he remembers. "Brown skin and hair way down to her hip. I was always crazy about long hair, you know." "Come on, Eubie, and let's play," begged Hoppy. "Ain't nobody in the world can beat you playing." "Yes, they can," sobbed the heartbroken Eubie, and he wouldn't play. That broke up the party and Edgar Dowell ended up with Eubie's girl. Later on, he also became the ragtime champion.

For a long time after that, the only music that Eubie would play was the music lessons which Margaret Marshall gave him. But the experience did one thing for him—it made him practice his scales because Edgar had beat him with his fingering technique. "He could play what we called 'walking bass,' " says Eubie. "They call it 'boogie woogie' now."

Around this time a man named Richard K. Fox, who owned the pink sporting paper called the *Police Gazette*, used to gather black performers from various towns and put on shows in Baltimore. In the summer time he put on such events as dancing contests, pie-eating contests and even watermelon eating contests. Once at the Lake Theater he featured a girl from Pittsburgh named Ragtime Mame. She may have been Pittsburgh's champion, but Edgar Dowell wiped her out as he had wiped out Eubie. "Boy, could he play the piano," Eubie exclaims. Later he played at Tom Smith's big hotel. People sometimes think that Eubie played for Smith, but it was actually Edgar.

CHAPTER 8

Eubie's first real job was playing the piano in Aggie Shelton's sporting house. Although she was supposed to be paying him three dollars per week, she hardly ever did, because she knew that he was making much more in tips. "This wasn't any peck-on-the-window come-on-in-boys type of house," says Eubie. "This was a swell house, a real five dollar house with swell furniture and everything." However, although he was now making all that money, he was still in short pants and had to rent a pair of long ones for twenty-five cents from the boy in the pool hall.

Needless to say, his parents knew nothing about his job. So each night after they had gone to sleep he would climb out of his window onto the shed, hop the back fence, get his long pants from the pool hall and then proceed on to Aggie's. "Boy, little as I was, [the pants] came way up to here," grins Eubie, pointing to a spot high on his chest. His father woke up at five o'clock to go to work, however, so Eubie always had to be sure to make it back before then.

But, as Eubie puts it, "murder will out." And one day one of the sisters of the church told his mother, "Em, little Eubie is playing 'pie-ano' at Aggie Shelton's house of ill fame." "How do you know?" Mrs. Blake demanded. "Don't nobody play like that, that ragtime, 'round here but Eubie," the sister answered. That evening, Mrs. Blake called Eubie in and began to question him. What could he say? So he admitted it, trying to sound as innocent as possible. "I'm going to kill you," she shouted. Crying, she asked the Lord why He had visited such a disgrace upon God-fearing Christians. Eubie had never seen her so angry and he was frightened. When his father came home from work she told him the story, repeating her determination to kill her son and thereby save him from the devil. "Now wait a minute, Em," said Mr. Blake. Taking Eubie out into the back yard, he asked, "Son, it this true?" Again Eubie admitted the truth, adding, "But I make so much money. Let me show you." So back they went through the house, past his mother, who was still crying, up the stairs to Eubie's room. Pulling back the rug, he showed his father the floor plastered with money. "You got all that money playing there?" asked his incredulous father. "Yes sir," replied the boy. "She don't pay me much, but I make it in tips for playing songs for the customers." There was about ninety dollars under that rug, more than Mr. Blake made in two months. Taking a fistful of the money, he went back downstairs, followed by a doubtful Eubie. "Let me handle this," he said to his son. "Em," he said, "it's true. The boy's got a room full of money he made playing at Aggie's house. [But] let's think this thing over. We've raised this boy to be a God-fearing Christian, haven't we?" "Yes," replied Mrs. Blake meekly. "That's what we tried to do." "Well," said Eubie's father, "with the raising we've given him, none of that sin won't rub off on a good Christian boy." At that, Eubie breathed a sigh of relief. He was saved!

Although Eubie was making all of that money, there was very little on which he could spend it. After all, he couldn't go into the saloons. Every Saturday he would spend about two dollars, taking his friends to the burlesque show and buying them some treats. The rest of the money he gave to his parents, buying his mother the nice things that she had always wanted.

His father had helped him to keep his job at Aggie's because he had always been very proud of his son's musical ability. Years later, when Eubie became well-known as a composer, his father would give him credit for practically every song that was written. Sitting on the curb with his cronies, the old man would swap tall tales about the Civil War. And whenever a marching band would come by, he would listen and say, "Hear that tune? My boy, that boy of mine, wrote that tune!" No matter what the tune was, he'd claim that Eubie had written it. That's how proud he was of his son.

Eubie's mother, however, being so religious, never stopped worrying about Eubie's soul. In 1902, when Eubie returned from Atlantic City, he took her to Ford's Theater to see a performance of black singers and dancers. When he asked her how she liked it, however, she answered, "It's lovely, Son. There's only one thing wrong. It would be so much nicer if they was doing this for Jesus." "Yes, Mamma," Eubie said without thinking, "but Jesus don't pay nothing." Upon hearing those words Mrs. Blake then created such an uproar that he had to rush her out of the theater and take her home!

Later on he played at Minnie Riley's "house," but although she had an even finer and more expensive place than Aggie Shelton, she didn't have the right "connections" with the police. After much harassment, they finally closed her down.

After that, Eubie took a job with Doc Frisbee's medicine show. Working with him were Preston Jackson, who sang and danced, Yellow Nelson and Slue-Foot Nelson, also dancers, and Knotty Bakerman, a comedian. Eubie played the melodeon, "a little musical contraption that folded and unfolded when you needed it." "Oh boy, we had a snappy show," recalls Eubie, "and the crowds loved it."

After playing all over Maryland, they went on into Pennsylvania, traveling in a horse-drawn wagon. It had a door that let down in back and that served as the stage. Coming into a town, they would first rest from their journey and then set up for the evening show, beating on a dishpan to attract the crowds. "Doc Frisbee was a super salesman," says Eubie. "He could mesmerize a crowd . . ." His medicine was supposed to cure warts, boils, acne, constipation, gout, fever, consumption and female complaints, and it sold like "hot cakes." He was good to his

32

entertainers, too, paying them fifty cents per day plus meals, except for Sundays, when he furnished only sandwiches in the evening.

Things went smoothly until one Sunday evening in Fairfield, Pennsylvania, when Preston rebelled. As Eubie says, "He was a smart aleck." (Dark-skinned, with fine features, straight black hair and little feet suitable for his outstanding dancing talents, he had all of the girls crazy about him.) Suddenly, sandwiches on Sundays were not good enough. Quitting his job, he demanded that the rest of the group quit with him and, like a bunch of fools, they did. There they were, stranded in Pennsylvania without any money with which to get home. But that didn't worry them. Young and crazy, they decided to walk back, pooling their money to buy some bread and some rolls of bologna. At first it seemed like fun, but pretty soon they got awfully tired of bologna and bread, and they got awfully angry at Preston for his stupid idea. But it was too late to turn back; all they could do was to go on. When they reached the mountains, Knotty Bakerman came back from buying some bread and told the others that a man had informed him of a short cut over the mountains. But, perhaps influenced by their regret over having listened to Preston, they refused to change their plans. Knotty, however, was adamant. "I'm going anyhow, whether you guys go or not," he insisted, and he set out alone with his share of the food. He went down the right trail, they went down the left one, and none of them ever heard of him again. For years they wondered what had ever become of him, but they never found out. As for the rest of them, they sang and danced their way home, going into the local saloon or pool hall in every little town they hit and putting on a show. The money that was pitched to them would feed them until they reached the next town, and that was the way they finally made it back to Baltimore.

After the medicine show fiasco, Eubie and Preston joined a show called "In Old Kentucky" as a dancing team. "I was a pretty good dancer myself," recalls Eubie, "but that Preston, he was the champ!" Leaving Baltimore on tour, they wound up in New York in 1902, playing in a place called the Academy of Music on Fourteenth Street. Eubie didn't like New York, however, just as later on he didn't like Europe. And so, although he had many offers to stay and work there, he left New York with Preston and returned to Baltimore.

CHAPTER 9

Eubie's first wife was named Avis Lee. Her grandfather was named Draper Lee and she was a society girl. When Eubie was eight or nine years old Avis used to take music lessons from a woman named Helen Cooper, a great pianist and singer who owned one of the two pianos in the neighborhood. (The only other piano was owned by a man named Hitch, who had a moving van wagon business on Jefferson Street, a block from Eubie's house. Eubie recalls that he "looked like a white man and talked dirty . . . in front of women.")

Eubie and Hoppy used to sit on the curb and watch Avis walk by. Although she was two years older than Eubie, she always looked young for her age, even in later years, and the fact of his youth did not deter Eubie one bit. "Hey, Hop," said Eubie one day as Avis approached, "here comes that young girl. I'm going to marry that girl!" "You don't know that girl," said Hop. "No, I don't know her," agreed Eubie, "but when I get big I'm gonna marry her." This was too much for Hoppy, and even though Eubie threatened to punch him, as soon as Avis got up to them Hop told her what Eubie had said. "You come here to me," said Avis to Eubie, and when he did she hit him over the head with the sharp part of her music book and knocked him out. But Eubie was undaunted, and when he came to he told her, "I'm going to marry you just the same." And he did, too, although it was twelve years later.

Several years passed and Eubie was already playing in sporting houses when he saw Avis again at a picnic at Round's Bay. When he had been in the sixth grade and she had been in the eighth, she had done his arithmetic for him. But he had never said much to her because she was what they then called "dicty" —rich and a little snobbish. (In fact, about fifteen or twenty years ago Eubie wrote a "rag," which he still plays in his concerts, about such people. He called it "Dicties on Seventh Avenue.") On this picnic was a young man named Eddie Nealy, who worked at the Goldfield Hotel and also at the Middle Section Club on Sunday nights waiting on tables. Like Eubie, he made good money and "dressed swell." He was tall and looked good in his clothes, but because he had a long head people called him "Eggie." His girlfriend was a friend of Avis', and the four of them spent the rest of the day together. After that, Eubie and Avis began to go out, and when three months had passed Eubie realized that he had fallen in love with her all over again. "You like that girl, don't you?" asked Eddie. "Why don't you marry her?" "I'm *gonna* marry her," replied Eubie. But it was not as simple as that.

Avis had never done a day's work in her life. Her family was "colored rich," and although she had never gone to college, she had had a fine education and had read a lot. According to Eubie, she was one of the five most beautiful women in Maryland. But she lived "uptown" on Druid Hill and Pressman's Street where the "swell Negroes" had their homes, whereas Eubie lived in the ghetto, played the piano in sporting houses and was also considered to be a pool shark. Eubie, however, was not to be deterred, and so one day he went to Avis' grandmother to ask for Avis' hand in marriage. "What do you do, Son?" the grandmother asked. He didn't tell her that he had been playing in sporting houses, of course, but she already knew it. And even his current job—playing at the Goldfield Hotel, where he had worked since its 1907 opening—was not quite fitting for the suitor of Lee Draper's granddaughter. "How much do you make a week?" she asked. "I make fifty-five dollars a week," answered Eubie, omitting the fifteen or twenty dollars a night which he made in tips. She didn't seem particularly impressed. "What is your background?", was her next question.

What a relief! At last he could impress her. "My mother and father belong to the Israel Baptist Church," he said proudly. "And my father and mother are what you call the pillars of the church." Avis' grandmother then wanted to know if Eubie had gone to Sunday School. "Oh, yes," was the answer. "Will you take care of my granddaughter?", she asked. "Sure I will," Eubie said. "I can take care of her. She ain't going to spend more than fifty-five dollars a week." Although he was now working for Ben Allen in Atlantic City and had to leave immediately, he promised her that if Avis accompanied him, until the wedding ceremony was performed he and Avis would occupy separate quarters. This statement further reassured her about the young man's intentions and she gave him her consent. So Avis went with Eubie to Atlantic City, and they were married by a preacher on their second night there.

Avis traveled with Eubie a lot. She understood what the life of a musician was like and she didn't mind. They went to Europe together, but although she loved Paris, Eubie was as unimpressed with the French city as he had been with London. "I didn't see enough colored people," Eubie says. "You know how it is. I want to see some of *us* sometimes." The only thing he liked about Paris was the sporting houses, where all the girls would come out naked.

Speaking of Avis, Eubie's voice assumes a softer, reverent tone. "You know," he says sadly, "she died of tuberculosis. It was in her family; her father and brother died of it also." Before she died, possibly to ease the symptoms of her illness— or to ease her own fears—she became a secret drinker. For a long time Eubie was unaware of this fact, but he finally found out through his friend Romaine Johns. At the time, Romaine was living with Eubie and Avis and tending bar in Harlem for an Italian man, who was only paying Romaine thirty-five dollars a week. ("Those guys owned most of the bars in Harlem in those days," recalls Eubie.) Since "everybody" in show business—black and white—knew Romaine, when they came to Harlem they would visit the place where he was working. For this reason Romaine figured that he deserved a raise, but when he asked his boss about it, the man refused. What could Romaine do? He couldn't quit; where would he go? So, since he couldn't get the money he wanted, he began to steal the bar's whiskey. Every night he brought home a fifth of one-hundred-proof Old Granddad, until pretty soon the bottom drawer of his dresser was full of bottles. He would keep one bottle open on top of the dresser, and he and Eubie would drink from it often. One morning, however, when he and Eubie were having a drink, a strange look came over his face as he downed his shot. "What's the matter with this whiskey, Romaine?" asked Eubie. "I really don't know for sure, Pop," Romaine answered, "But if it's what I think, I don't want you to get mad at what I'm going to say." He then went to Avis' room and confronted her. "Mom," he demanded, "have you been putting water in my whiskey?" When she began to explain, he cut her off. "You know you can share anything in the world I've got . . . Have all you want, any time you want to. But goddamit, don't put no water in my whiskey." That was the only time Eubie ever heard Romaine speak harshly to Avis, because he loved her like a mother.

Later, when Avis died, Romaine was away. Eubie phoned him and said simply, "Mom is gone." "I'll be there," Romaine answered, and arrived that very night. "You take care of everything," said Eubie, who has never been very good at business matters. And Romaine did.

CHAPTER 10

Joe Gans, the boxer, was a long-time friend of Eubie's. His real name was Josephus Butts, and as children, he and Eubie played marbles together, although Joe was older. "I don't know how he became 'Joe Gans,' " says Eubie. Later, he and Eubie and Preston Jackson—the one who had gotten Eubie and his friends stranded in the Pennsylvania mountains—became close friends. In fact, they were inseparable. They wore identical turtleneck sweaters, and when a person saw one of the three, the other two were bound to be close by.

Although Gans was an excellent fighter, he was always broke. Even after he beat Frank Erne for the championship he was still making only three thousand dollars per fight, and he was paying for a fine new home for his stepmother. So Eubie and Preston carried him financially. But lack of money evidently meant nothing as far as his reputation was concerned, because he was a great ladies' man. As a matter of fact, he was married four times, although two of the marriages were annulled through the influence of Al Herford.

Eubie smiles as he recalls an incident connected with one of Joe's women. "She was just *one* of his girls, see," he emphasizes. One afternoon after leaving her house he sat down on the curb to wait for a streetcar. "Well, now I hear a lot about police brutality in the cities nowadays," says Eubie, "but let me tell you, there were some of the meanest, orneriest policemen in Baltimore of anyplace in the world, and some of them would do anything to you." On that particular day, as Gans was sitting there he was approached by a policeman who demanded, "Nigger, what are you doing sitting there?" "I'm just sitting here waiting for the streetcar," answered Gans. The policeman was a huge man, whereas Gans stood about five feet six inches tall and never weighed over one hundred and fifty pounds in his life. "Get up, Nigger!" shouted the policeman. "Stand up when you talk to me." When Gans stood up, the officer struck at him with his club, but the blow just grazed Gan's arm. Just then a police sergeant who had been watching the scene came rushing up. "What's going on here?", he demanded. "Why, this nigger got smart with me," answered the policeman, "and I'm going to teach him a lesson." But the sergeant knew Gans. "Wait a minute," he said, "this man is a gentleman. Don't you know that's Joe Gans, the lightweight champion of the world?" At that, the big mean policeman just fainted dead away!

When Gans fought Frank Erne for the first time and Erne butted his eye out, Gans quit and lost the match by default. He became very despondent then and talked of never fighting again, but he had no choice. He couldn't do anything else. Like Eubie, he only had one trade, only one way in which to make money.

When Eubie and Preston returned to Baltimore in 1902, Joe Gans was there, too. But although he was winning all of his fights now, he still wasn't making any money. Barney Schrieber, a big bookmaker out of Pimlico, and Al and Maurice Herford had Gans all sewed up; *they* were making the money instead of *him*. Joe Tipman was a good fighter then too, and he never made much either, but he was never a champion like Gans was.

In those days a man named Kid North worked for Barney Schrieber as a "betting commissioner" in Baltimore's black section. He was also one of Gans' seconds in his important fights. Occasionally he would take a chance when Gans was fighting and take on a lot of outside bets which Barney wasn't backing. This was very dangerous, of course, because if Gans lost, the Kid had no money to cover the bets which he had made. If Gans won, though, the Kid cleaned up. During one such fight, Gans was trying to prolong the action and make things look good when his opponent got in a lucky punch and knocked him down. That really hurt Joe, and when he came back to his corner, the Kid made things worse by saying, "What's the matter? What you let him knock you down for, Joe?" " 'Cause he's got two fists," Gans answered. "If you think you can do better, you go out there and fight him the next round!" He knew about the Kid's bets and was purposely trying to scare him, but the Kid didn't know it and he panicked. "Come on, Joe," he pleaded, "you can take him next round." Gans shook his head. "I donno, Kid, I donno," he said. "My God, man," gasped the frightened Kid. "don't talk like that! You're the great Joe Gans. You've got to whip him. If you don't, ole Kid has got to leave Baltimore or get killed." But Gans carried on the fight for another round or two, having fun at the Kid's expense, before he finally decided to end the fight with a knock-out.

CHAPTER 11

Eubie's friendship with Gans lasted for many years, but it finally came to a sudden and bitter end. At this time Eubie was going to Atlantic City every year, playing in places like Ben Allen's, the Belmont and the Boathouse. After the season closed in September, however, he would return to Baltimore. He was a great ladies' man in those days. "I couldn't help it," he smiles. "They were all kinds all 'round me." But then, in spite of the number of women around him, he fell in love with a lady who was a "friend of the boys." He knew what she was but he just couldn't help himself. He was hooked, and nothing his pals could say would change his mind. Finally Joe Gans decided to break it up for good. He did, too, but in the process he ruined a long-time friendship forever.

As close as Eubie was to Gans, he began to sense a tension growing between them, but he was unable to pinpoint its source. One evening they were at the bar in Greenfield's Saloon when Gans bought a round of drinks. As they lifted their glasses, however, a gambler named Joe Prentice turned to Eubie and said, "I wouldn't drink with that guy Gans if I were you." That really puzzled Eubie and the feeling of tension mounted, but he still didn't know what was wrong. Things finally came to a head one night in a gambling house on Lexington Street. A group of "big shot gamblers" had a poker game upstairs. Downstairs was a bar and a crap game run by a man named Mr. Zebbs. Eubie laughs as he recalls the man. "He was an old guy, black as coal, and he called everybody that came in there a black S.O.B. Everybody, even the big white gamblers, who came around the game were black S.O.B.'s to him."

Eubie had heard about the game upstairs, so he went to Mr. Zebbs to borrow twenty-five dollars. "You're a fool about women and now you really are a fool to sit in that game upstairs," scoffed the old man, but he gave him the money. Now Eubie had fifty dollars with which to bet. Gans was in the game, as were two big white gamblers and a black gambler named Thompson. Thompson was a rather special man around Baltimore; he had some sort of inside political influence. He was the only black man at that time who could eat in the railroad station dining room. Once in awhile he would take Eubie with him and they'd have the finest steaks a man could eat. But by himself Eubie couldn't even get served there.

When Eubie got his chips, Gans looked at him and said, "What you doing in this game, juvenile?" Eubie was puzzled; Gans had never spoken to him like that before. "I've got fifty bucks worth of fish," Eubie answered. "That's what I'm doing in here." "You ain't got no business in this game and I'm going to teach you a lesson," said Gans. But Eubie just laughed. For several hands he didn't get any good cards, but suddenly he got two jacks and he opened for five dollars. Gans, to Eubie's left, called and raised the pot twelve dollars and fifty cents. But Eubie, knowing that Gans was a great bluffer, called the raise and stayed in. By now everybody had folded but him and Gans. Looking at him, Gans repeated his mockery, "Why don't you get out, juvenile? You can't beat me. I told you I was going to teach you a lesson." Eubie didn't reply, except to ask for three cards. It didn't help. Gans then asked the dealer for four cards, with the first one face up. That first card was a queen. "Washed away, juvenile," he sneered. "Now don't you wish you were dead?" Angry now, Eubie bet twenty-five dollars. "Call it and raise all you got in front of you," dared Gans, laughing wildly. Eubie put in his remaining money and Gans turned up two queens. The game was over; Eubie was broke. As Gans raked in the pot, he began to laugh like a crazy man.

"Didn't I tell you I'd clean you?" he shouted. "As lucky as
_____'s stuff is to me, don't you know you can't never beat
me?" And he called Eubie's girl's name. Eubie jumped up from
the table, sick and outraged, challenging Gans to a fight, but
the other men held him back. Gans went on down to the bar,
still laughing, but he became so hysterical that the men had to
call a carriage and take him home. Then they called for Doc
Lucas, a "quack" who had been expelled from medical school
because of "bad character" and gambling. He treated all of the
pimps, prostitutes and gamblers, however, and he made a lot of
money. Doc gave Gans a shot but when it wore off he went
into hysterics again. It took some time for him to regain his
equilibrium. But his friendship with Eubie was destroyed forever.

Someone asks, "But later you opened his Goldfield Hotel,
didn't you, Eubie?" "Sure, sure I did," Eubie answers. "I didn't
hate Joe. I just didn't trust him or care for him anymore. Besides, I got fifty-five dollars a week salary and that was good pay
in those days." Eubie's loss of affection for Gans was one-sided,
however; Gans continued to be fond of Eubie until he died.
Both he and Eubie loved stewed tomatoes, and when Joe opened
the Goldfield, he had stewed tomatoes on the menu every day.
"Don't sell all the stewed tomatoes," he would tell his wife.
"Save some for old Eubie, but don't tell him I told you to do
it." She did tell Eubie, of course, but it didn't matter. Eubie
could just never feel any more warmth for his old friend, no
matter how hard Gans tried to make it up to him.

In spite of his success, however, Joe Gans had a tragic life.
His spectacular prowess in that poker game with Eubie notwith-
standing, he really wasn't much of a gambler, although he
thought that he was.

When he fought Kid Herman in Tonopah, Nevada, the pro-
moter sent him a thousand dollars in advance for traveling ex-

penses. But on the way to Tonopah he and Kid North stopped off in Chicago. That was his mistake; Teenan and Give-a-Damn Jones talked him into gambling with them and some other big-time South Side gamblers, and Gans lost the whole thousand dollars. He couldn't even get out of town until Al Herford wired him another thousand!

Gans also fancied himself a great casino player, and after he opened the Goldfield he and a little Jewish gambler called Jew Abie would play casino every day at the oyster bar. "It would be a great show to watch!", remembers Eubie. Abie would catch Gans cheating and scream, "Goddamit Gans, you ain't playing fair!" "Don't cuss in here," Gans would shout back. "Don't you see my wife over there behind the bar? You know goddamn well I didn't try to cheat you!" "I do respect Mrs. Gans," Abie would shout, "but goddamit, you know you were cheating." And on and on they would go.

When Battling Joe Nelson was claiming that he, as the white champion, was the *real* lightweight champion of the world, Joe was angry and surly all of the time. Finally the first Gans-Nelson fight took place. When news of Gans' victory flashed over the wire that afternoon, all of the black and many of the white "sports" in Baltimore went wild. "Talk about a celebration," says Eubie. "You ain't seen nothing like it. Why, Gans could've had anything in town, as least till the novelty wore off."

After that fight, Gans fought and beat Kid Herman in Tonopah. He also beat Jimmy Britt, although Britt broke his elbow. Then he knocked out Bart Blackburn, Spike Robson and Rudy Unholz. But even though he could still punch as well as ever, he was a sick man. He had tuberculosis, the dread disease which was later to take the life of Avis Blake. He should have been in the hospital, but he went on fighting.

He had gained weight also and this put him into the welter-weight category, but he couldn't make any money this way. So he accepted one last fight with Nelson, even though he knew that losing the weight to put him back into the lightweight class-ification was going to kill him. The fight took place in Colma, California, in September, 1908. Only a small crowd was there, about five thousand people, and Joe fought for nineteen rounds before his strength left him. In the final round, the twenty-first, he hardly even struck a blow. He was finished. Two years later, at the age of thirty-five, Joe Gans was dead.

Eubie was playing in Atlantic City when he got the news of Gans' death. Although he was very sorry, he had never gotten over what Gans had done to him, not even now, when he was a successful entertainer with a young and beautiful wife. He just couldn't help himself. On the day of the funeral he was going to stay in Atlantic City and work as usual. But Avis was horrified, even though she knew the story about Eubie's former girlfriend and Joe. "Listen," she said, "if you go to work and don't go to that funeral, when you come home I won't be here." Eubie tried to argue with her, but her mind was made up. And he knew that she would carry out her threat. So he caught the train from Atlantic City to Baltimore. When he got there, how-ever, he couldn't get no closer than a block from the church. "Man," he says, "you never saw such a crowd around a church!" And the funeral procession looked as if it would never end.

CHAPTER 12

In 1903 Eubie was working again in Baltimore at a saloon on Chestnut Street called Greenfield's. Working with another piano player named Big Head Wilbur, he started to compose more music. "Boy, it was a great time," Eubie says. "Pimps, hustlers and fancy ladies all over the place."

Leaving Baltimore, he again tried New York, but again he couldn't stay, and so once more he came back home, this time to work at the Middle Section Club on Lexington Street. "Things were jumping then," he remembers, "and life was sweet for me. It was a great feeling to be able to take care of my mother and father and see that they wanted for nothing."

While working at the Middle Section Club, Eubie also started to fill in for his friend Big Jimmy Green, who played at a club owned by a man named Coots Jones. Big Jimmy had taken ill, and when he died Eubie wrote the song, "Poor Jimmy Green" in his memory. "Boy, Jimmy was a swell piano player," Eubie recalls, "and that mustache of his was the biggest handlebar job you ever saw."

In 1907, Joe Gans and a man named Eddie Meyers brought Coots' place, tore it down and replaced it with the Goldfield Hotel. "I guess you'd call it early American slum clearance," chuckles Eubie. The hotel is gone now, a grocery store standing in its place, but the name "Goldfield Hotel still remains in the cement in front of the door. "At least they have left that much of the memory of Joe Gans," he reflects.

The Goldfield was the "swellest" place ever owned by blacks in Baltimore and on opening night Eubie and a musician named One Leg Willie were the piano players. Willie had been trained at the Boston Conservatory of Music and he had won the final competitions there in his last year at the school. But instead of giving it to him, the school authorities had called him in and explained that although he had won the award, he couldn't have it because he was "colored." It broke Willie's heart. After that, he stopped trying to play "white" music and took up ragtime. But he couldn't forget his classical training, and he used this knowledge as a base for his playing. One of his most spectacular numbers was Sousa's "Stars and Stripes Forever." First he would play it in march time and then he would repeat it in ragtime. It was a tremendous hit.

Opening night at the Goldfield was the greatest event which had ever occurred in the Baltimore of those times. Carriages lined up for blocks, and the white "sports" and "swells" filled the place to overflowing. Night after night the champagne flowed. Whiskey was fifty cents a shot, which was very expensive back then, and there was excellent food, too. The club finally got so popular that some white entertainment people forced through a city ordinance barring blacks and whites from mixing socially in Baltimore. But that happened much later. It was here that Eubie was playing when he proposed to Avis.

One of the bartenders at the Goldfield was a man named Daniel "Sleepy" Sims. At one time he had gone with Joe Gans' wife's sister, although no-one knew it when he was working at the Goldfield. Sleepy and Eubie were pals, and when the bar closed in the morning the two men would, as Eubie puts it, go out "hookshopping," going to different girls' houses and buying drinks. Eubie would soon go home to bed but Sleepy would just keep on going. At six o'clock, however, there he would be behind the bar, white coat on, as fresh-looking as ever. Although Sleepy was noted for his cursing, as soon as he donned that white coat, his personality changed. Instantly professional, he called everybody "Sir" and "Mister"; even Eubie.

One night a white man came in and told Sleepy to set up drinks for everybody at the bar. The word got out and soon the bar was crowded, but still the man kept buying drinks. He, himself, however, wasn't drinking. When the other men lifted their glasses, he would put his own down on the bar. Finally he said to Sleepy, "I donno, it's something about you I like. What is your name?" "My name is Dan Sims," said Sleepy, "but they call me 'Sleepy.'" "Well," said the white man, "we'll have a drink together." Then he repeated, "You know, I . . I don't know why, but I just like you." As Sleepy began to take his drink, the man asked him if he had noticed that he had not been drinking with the other men. Sleepy *had* noticed it, of course, but he pretended that he had not. The man then asked Sleepy if he was curious as to the reason, and when Sleepy admitted his curiosity, the man said, "Well, now, I'll tell you. I told you I liked you, didn't I? I'm going to do something now I never done in my life before. I'm going to take a drink with a nigger!" At those words, Sleepy picked up his glass and smashed it on the tile floor behind the bar. "Well," he said, "I'll be godamned if I'm going to start you off!" And Sleepy didn't drink with him.

CHAPTER 13

During the summers in those days Eubie would go to Atlantic City to play at places like Kelly's, the Belmont Club, and Big Brownie and Ben Allen's Boathouse, making four or five dollars a night plus "great tips." "Did you ever see a brownie in a picture?", Eubie asks. "A brownie had a great big body with little tiny legs, wearing fur coats and little thin legs and pants. Well, that's how Ben Allen looked." He used to buy half sides of beef and feed all of the "hustlers" who were down on their luck and "couldn't even get back to Philadelphia." Byron Hudson used to do the same thing in New York.

Jack Johnson, the fighter about whom the movie "The Great White Hope" was made, was around then. He had no money and couldn't get any fights, so Ben "fed him and bankrolled him" for several years. Finally, however, Jack's luck changed. In Philadelphia he knocked out Flip Simons in three or four rounds. And later, after he beat Jim Jeffries, he returned one day to Atlantic City, driving his racing car and accompanied by his manager, George Little, and his white girlfriend. And the first place he came to was the Boathouse.

Big Brownie saw them coming and ran ahead to warn his partner. "Ben," he shouted, "Jack Johnson's in town, and they've got a big crowd following him and he's on his way here to see you. But he's got that white woman in the car with him." And Ben panicked. You see, back then, a black man could do anything within reason on the "black" side of Atlantic Avenue and get straightened out with the law. But once he got into trouble on the "other side," he had no chance; he would get "lifetime." And on one thing the law was very definite—it did not want a white woman to "hang around" the black side of Atlantic Avenue. Even—or especially—if she was with Jack Johnson.

50

When Jack Johnson drove up, he honked his horn and yelled for Ben to come out. "Go back, you black S.O.B. and take that white woman away," Ben hollered back. "But Ben, I want to pay you your money," Jack protested. It was to no avail; Ben was adamant. He would not let Jack come into the Boathouse, and he refused to take his money.

CHAPTER 14

Madison Reed was Eubie's first partner. He was what was called in those days a "wench comedian," and he also wrote songs, including one called "Make Me a Pallet on the Floor," which Eubie still occasionally hears played on T.V. He had worked with the Bryant Brothers before coming to Baltimore in 1902 or 1903, when he and Eubie began to work together down by the river at Kelly's Park.

In Atlantic City, when Eubie and Madison were performing at the Belmont Club, they used to sing "Alexander's Ragtime Band" from ten to twenty times a night. All of the waitresses would form a chain behind Madison and they would dance around the room singing while Eubie played the piano.

Irving Berlin would come to Atlantic City often and Sophie Tucker would bring him to the club. "He was the saddest looking fellow I've ever seen," said Eubie. "He looked so thin and hungry that I felt sorry for him." "Alexander's Ragtime Band" was his favorite song. "Hey, Eubie, play my tune," he would say. And Eubie would play it. It appeared to be everyone else's favorite tune, too, at that time. In fact, it was requested so often that Eubie got sick of playing it. "But I can't play it anymore," says Eubie wistfully. "I wish I could play it now like I could then. I was strong then. It takes a lot of strength to play ragtime."

Berlin was also a good friend of pianist Lukie Johnson. ("Everybody said he looked just like me," recalls Eubie. "He had a bald head just like me.") At one time Lukie worked with Berlin in the Bowery at a place called Nigger Mike's. Years later in New York, when Lukie would lose all of his money gambling, he would come to Eubie asking for a loan.

"I'll give it back when the Old Man comes back to town," he would promise. The "Old Man" was Berlin, who always gave Lukie money because he liked him so much.

For years there had been a rumor circulating that Lukie Johnson or some other black man had really written Irving Berlin's music. Finally curiosity got the best of Eubie and one night he questioned Lukie about it. "Does Irving Berlin buy his tunes from you?", he asked. "Did he write 'Alexander's Ragtime Band' or did you write it?" "I wish to God I *had* written that song," answered Lukie. "Irving Berlin don't buy no tunes from me. He writes them himself."

Several years ago Irving Berlin appeared at an ASCAP show. Coming out on the stage, he announced, "Now I'm going to sing for you a new song I've just completed." After the applause died down, he added, "Now I want you to know that I wrote this song myself. The little colored boy didn't write it!" That brought the house down.

George M. Cohan used to come to the Belmont, too, when he was in town. He would let Eubie play his songs and, as Eubie says, "We'd have a ball." He once told Eubie, "Eubie, never monkey with a success. When you find a partner you can trust and work in harmony with, never change him." Some years later, when Eubie met his lifetime partner, Noble Sissle, he was to remember those words. Cohan also told him, "Never write for the other writers; write for the public," and, "Never write over the public's head. Write simply so that the little working girl can carry your tune." And Eubie was to follow that advice, with one exception. That was when he wrote "Memories of You" for Minta Cato. Minta had a voice range that covered an octave and a half, and she could hit the "A" above staff with perfect ease. However, since most singers could not reach that note, Eubie intended to write in an optional lower note

53

for others' voices. In the rush for publication, though, he forgot, and afterwards he just decided not to change it.

CHAPTER 15

Eubie first met pianist Willie the Lion, whom he called "Old Braggadocio," when he was playing at the Belmont Club in Atlantic City. When he left to go back to Baltimore in 1914 or 1915, Willie took over his job. "The Lion was a great pianist," says Eubie fondly, "For my part, I ain't heard nobody play like him. I've been playing the piano for my living since the Fourth of July, 1901. And I've been around all the best pianists in the country. And I'm telling you, the Lion would wipe all these kids out that I hear now."

Their friendship proved to be an enduring one. Several years ago, Rudi Blesh, co-author of *They All Played Ragtime,* invited Eubie and Willie to one of his concerts at Newport. The first performer was a pianist named Don Lambert. They had never heard of him, and he looked like he was about to fall asleep while he was playing, but he could really play. The crowd went wild. Willie and Eubie had to follow him, and Eubie, thinking of how Edgar Dowell had wiped him out at that Baltimore lawn party years ago, was worried. Willie, however, was not impressed, even when Lambert played "Tea for Two" with his right hand and another song with his left at the same time. Eubie got up first and played "The Charleston Rag" and "Tricky Fingers," a rag which Eubie had composed in Baltimore to show up Big Head Wilbur and the other "sharks" around town when the competition was tough. He got a standing ovation. Then Willie got up and delivered a short lecture on ragtime and jazz. By that time he had gotten himself together, and he then sat down and played. He got a standing ovation also. "I tell you, you couldn't beat Willie," Eubie says. "He was the greatest."

Unfortunately, their friendship became a little strained when

Eubie's album, *Eighty-Six Years of Eubie Blake,* came out. When Willie had written his book, he had mentioned Eubie and given him credits. When Eubie's album came out, however, Willie was completely omitted. "I was sorry," says Eubie, "[but] I just couldn't help it. I simply went to the sessions and recorded." Not included in the planning of the album, he had had nothing to do with the selection of material. But Willie was still hurt, and on two subsequent occasions, he snubbed Eubie in public.

CHAPTER 16

"We had some real characters in Baltimore in those days," Eubie recalls. One of the strangest was an old school friend, nicknamed "Bayview" after the mental institution of that name. Married to an ex-girlfriend of Eubie's named Mattie, he was a compulsive gambler. At one time he worked in a fish market, and after work he would come into the Goldfield to drink, smelling of fish. Finally, however, he won a couple hundred dollars and opened his own market across from the hotel, stocking fish, vegetables, and live terrapins—a foot and half high.

Since he was now making money, he decided that he could afford to replace the two missing teeth in his wife's mouth. So he sent her to the dentist and had her fitted with gold ones. But the strange part was that he had the dentist fix them so that they could be screwed in or out at will.

One Christmas Day, Bayview was shooting craps at the Goldfield and lost all of his money. And, since Gans and Eddie Meyers, one of the Goldfield's owners, refused to loan him any, he began to pawn things. Across the street was a pawn shop owned by a Jewish man named Louie. All of the big-time gamblers could pawn things there when they were down on their luck because Louie knew that they would soon hit a winning streak and redeem their possessions. Besides, he was making twenty-five cents on the dollar.

From the Goldfield, Eddie and his friends watched Bayview going back and forth, from his house and store to the pawnshop and then to the hotel. And he still kept losing. Mattie was standing there crying, "Bay, don't strip my house. Don't do this." But he just told her to shut up. Finally, his entire house and shop were bare. He had even pawned the terrapins. So back he went into his house, unscrewed his wife's gold teeth, and

57

pawned those, too. The last thing that he carried over to Louie's was the hot turkey out of the kitchen stove. "Honest to God!" exclaims Eubie, forstalling any comments from disbelievers. But somehow, he managed to win everything back at the end, terrapins, teeth, and all.

Eddie Meyers, who was one of Eubie's closest friends, also ran a poker game upstairs at the Middle Section Club. One Sunday afternoon, when the club was crowded with "nice respectable" church ladies who had sneaked over for a drink, a man fell asleep with his feet in the aisle. Since Eddie had to pass him carrying drinks, he woke the man and asked him to move his feet. But the man just cursed at him. The bar was full of ladies, and Eddie didn't want to start an argument in front of them, so he tried to ignore the incident. Finally, however, the inevitable happened. The man put out his feet to stretch just at the time that Eddie was walking by with a tray full of drinks, and of course he tripped and dropped them. Eddie at last had had enough. In anger, he slapped the man and knocked him out.

When the man woke up, he asked Eddie who had slapped him, and when Eddie said that it had been he, the man proceeded to hit Eddie, and a fight ensued. In the middle of the fight, a friend of Eddie's, thinking to help him, rushed in and knocked the troublemaker out again. But once more he came to and began throwing punches. And once more he was knocked out, this time by Eddie again. When the man woke up for the third time, however, he had evidently had enough, because he simply got up and left quietly.

For a week, nobody saw the man around, but on Saturday night, he returned to the club. Anticipating trouble, Eddie was ready for him, but to his immense surprise, the man just wanted Eddie to go upstairs and have a drink with him. "Ed," he said, "You're the guy who stopped me from getting on a Saturday night." And the two of them got to be the best of friends.

In Atlantic City there were some characters too. Two of them were Andrew Terry, a young black man, and Kitey, a young white man. Although Kitey was bigger than Andrew, he could never beat him in a fight. And although they were actually the best of friends, Kitey never gave up trying to win. People would see Kitey coming down the street toward the bar and when he would walk in the men would say, "O God, here comes Kitey! He's gonna start another fight!" And sure enough, he would. Andrew kept trying to duck Kitey, but to no avail. If he tried to run out the side door, Kitey would corner him and convince him to go back in and let him buy a few drinks. But then, of course, he would end up starting another fight. It went on for years, until they were both too old to fight, but Andrew beat Kitey every time.

"That's how fellows were in those days," muses Eubie. "Guys fought just to see who was the best man. There wasn't all this . . . shooting, stabbing, and cutting that goes on today. Nowadays, you're even scared to look at anybody in most cases."

Another Atlantic City character was a man called Applejack, a constant drinker who used to run errands for Ben Allen. He pushed a rolling chair down the boardwalk in the summertime. The only problem was that whenever Ben sent him on an errand to buy something for him, Applejack would always add on something for himself—silk shirts, neckties, socks, it didn't matter what it was. Ben finally had had enough, and one day he stopped speaking to Applejack. It was winter now and Applejack had no other source of income. Crushed, he got drunk, climbed up on the roof of the four-story apartment house across the street from the Boathouse, where Ben's nephew Johnnie lived, and threatened to jump. "Tell Ben if he don't speak to me, I'm going to jump," he hollered. "I love him. He takes care of me." A crowd soon gathered, and a gambler named Diamond ran to get Ben. "Don't jump, Joe," Ben pleaded. "I'm three weeks

behind in your insurance. I'll speak to you if you come down."
"No," said Applejack. "Take an oath." So Ben did, while
Diamond sneaked up behind Applejack and pulled him down.
And when they got him to the door, Ben jumped on Applejack
and almost killed him.

CHAPTER 17

In Eubie's early days in Baltimore he was a "pool shark." But he never did any hustling; he never tried to disguise his playing prowess. Others did, however—those to whom Eubie refers as "lemon pool players." Going into a pool hall, a lemon player would play so badly that everyone watching would be sure that he was an amateur. After being challenged to a game, however, he would suffer a few initial losses and then suddenly make a remarkable recovery, sometimes winning a substantial amount of money.

One such hustler was a man named Charlie "Lucky" Roberts. Short, fat and dumb-looking, he was actually what Eubie calls a "slicker." He would go down to the white neighborhood, go into a bar with a pool table, and, in his dumbest voice, ask to play the piano. Of course the bartender would say "Yes." After playing for awhile and passing the hat, he would go to put the money away, and in the process would flash a "Michigan bankroll"—bills on the outside and toilet paper inside. Naturally, he would end up playing pool, since everyone would then be determined to take away his money. And naturally he would eventually end up winning.

One day when Eubie was talking to the bartender in the Goldfield, three men came in and told him about Lucky's playing in the white bars. "I know he's playing lemon pool," one man said, although he himself, being black, had only been able to watch Lucky's games through the windows. "You tell him don't play down there. Those guys will kill him if they find out he's a lemon pool player. They eat up Negroes down there!"

A few nights later when Lucky came into the Goldfield, Eubie questioned him about it. "I make more money playing pool than you do," Lucky explained. "You play a hard game. I ain't gonna play that hard. I look for suckers." "Charlie," said Eubie, "if they ever catch you, they'll kill you." But although Lucky would promise not to go back to the white bars, he always did.

Lucky was really an excellent pianist. He could read music and play in all the keys, and he had played in all of the popular spots in New York. Every winter he would take four or five singers and go down to Florida to play at private affairs. One of his colleagues was Broadway Jones, who later worked with Eubie during World War I when Eubie's partner Noble Sissle was overseas. The rich people loved his voice and he had his own clientele down there, all millionaires.

One night a millionaire asked Lucky to get Broadway to sing for a party. Lucky got one hundred dollars and so did Broadway, as he always did. But when Lucky went to distribute the money, he only gave Broadway fifty dollars, and no matter how Broadway argued, he could not get Lucky to admit that he was cheating him.

A short time later Broadway got a job, and this millionaire wanted Lucky to play the piano. When the party was over and it was time to be paid, Broadway asked for cash, and asked the man to pay him in front of Lucky. "O.K.," said the man, and gave Broadway two hundred dollars. When they went outside, however, all that Broadway gave to Lucky was fifty dollars, claiming that all he had been given was one hundred dollars. "You're lying to me," said Lucky. "You did it to me," replied Broadway. "Now I'm doing it to you." And although they remained friends, they never worked together again.

Later, Jerome Kern went down to Florida and heard a lot of black singers, and he decided to write the musical "Show Boat." And having heard Broadway sing, he wrote the song "Old Man River" expressly for his voice. When it came time to cast the show, Kern sent to Harlem for Broadway. At that time Broadway was making a lot of money on his own and wasn't particularly impressed with this. So he went to his friend Romaine Johns—the same Romaine who discovered Avis' secret drinking—and asked him to be his agent. "Ask him for five hundred dollars a week," he said. "What's your lowest figure?" asked Romaine. "Three hundred and not a penny lower," answered Broadway. So Romaine went down to Kern and quoted Broadway's figures. "You fellows must be crazy," said the old man. "Why man, I can probably get Caruso for that money!" So Romaine came back to Harlem and told his friend about the rejection. But Broadway didn't care. He could make one hundred dollars or more a night just singing at private parties. Furthermore, if he had taken the part he would have to rehearse and show up to work at regular intervals. So that was the end of Broadway's career on Broadway and Romaine's career as an agent. Kern had also heard Jules Bledsoe sing, so he auditioned him next and Bledsoe got the part instead. And he was a smash hit, too, which just goes to show that no performer, regardless of how good he is, is really indispensable.

CHAPTER 18

Besides the pool table, another big attraction in the bars of Eubie's early youth was gambling, and many of Eubie's friends were big-time gamblers.

When Eubie was playing at the Boathouse in Atlantic City, two of his gambler friends were Caspar Holstein and Bert Griffin, who was also from Baltimore. "I can see him now, in memory," says Eubie of Caspar. "He always wore custom-made shoes; they were split down the middle. He was a fine dresser, too. He had an air about him; you know how big gamblers are. They seem to exhibit a feeling of great self-confidence and ego."

One day Caspar and Bert got into a crap game with three white men from New York whom no-one had ever seen before. They had a new trick which they had brought with them, and they had come down to Atlantic City to clean the place out. And indeed they appeared to be doing just that. The dice did amazing things for them, and they were breaking Caspar, Bert, and everyone else around the crap table. "Oh man, you never saw anything like that in your life," says Eubie. "Why, they could almost make the dice talk."

Finally someone sent for Hus Robinson. He was from Baltimore, too, and was the cleverest man with dice that Eubie had ever seen. Hus came down to the Boathouse and watched the three white men for awhile. "What are they doing, Hus?" he was asked. "I don't know," he answered. "I ain't seen that stuff before." He knew some white men around Atlantic City, so he went to them and asked them if they knew what the strangers were doing. "They're pad rolling the dice," he was told. "They're rolling them on a padded pool table." So Hus went home, padded his kitchen table, and practiced.

The strangers had already cleaned Caspar and his friends—

Bert, Black Diamond, Big Boy Prattis, and the others—but they still had not gotten to Ben Allen and another gambler named Fitzgerald, who were the two richest men around. So they came back the next day. Now, however, Hus was ready for them. "And man," chuckles Eubie, "he not only had the dice walking and talking, they were pulling up chairs for each other!" At first the strangers thought that he was just making some lucky passes. But they had to keep playing, and they kept losing. Whenever they slacked up on their bets, though, Hus would let the dice pass to them to allay their suspicions. But when the dice got back to him, he would do it again. Finally, of course, Hus and his friends won, and Caspar and all of the Atlantic City gamblers got their money back.

Caspar and the other gamblers carried their money with them in chamois bags that were attached to their suspenders and hung down inside their trousers. And they would bet on anything. When Nelson beat Gans in that second fight, Caspar must have lost nearly two thousand dollars and the other black gamblers did, too. But they kept on betting.

In those days in Atlantic City, two girls—Mary Stafford and Virginia Smith—both sang in clubs, and on a cool night they could be heard five or six blocks away. And they sounded just alike. Caspar and his friends would be standing around listening to the singing when one of them would say, "That's Mary Stafford singing." "That ain't no Mary Stafford; that's Virginia Smith singing," another would counter. So they would bet fifty or one hundred dollars and then go down the street to see who was actually singing, and the loser would have to pay off.

Those men would even bet on such things as the color of the next horse to come by or the sex of the next customer to enter the bar. They were just natural gamblers, and Caspar was the head of them all.

Years later Caspar became a big man in Harlem, with plenty

of money and women. But he wasn't satisfied. For some reason he always wanted to be president of the Elks Lodge. But try as he might, he just couldn't oust the current Grand Exalted Ruler, Finley Wilson. Wilson was too slick and shrewd, and he knew more old parliamentary tricks than the politicians in Washington. He was unbeatable. And although Caspar never gave up, he just couldn't make it.

When the white mob came into Harlem to take over the numbers game, they kidnapped Caspar and held him for fifty thousand dollars ransom. It was rumored that he paid off, too. Another big black numbers man was Joe Tanner. He owned apartment buildings on Riverside Drive in the white neighborhood, but when he collected his rents he had to go to the basement. He may have been the owner, but he was still black! When the whites took over the numbers, Joe got disgusted and quit. Going to the police station, he told the captain, "If any of my numbers men get locked up after six o'clock today, don't come to me. I'm quitting today." "You can't quit," said the captain. "You'll get killed." "I ain't scared of nobody," replied Joe, "and I'm quitting." And he did. Nine years later he died of cancer.

CHAPTER 19

In his long lifetime, Eubie has known so many great musicians. "They used to call me the greatest," he says. "But there was so much tough piano competition in towns like Philadelphia. They don't make them like those guys anymore. I know if I keep repeating this they'll say that I'm just another oldtimer trying to put down the young piano men. But I swear it's not so." The only exception which Eubie makes is Oscar Peterson. "He's the greatest," Eubie says. "In fact, he overpowers a piano. He's in a class by himself."

One of the greatest pianists whom Eubie knew was Joe Stewart. He could "read and play anything." Another great was Sammy Stewart, who came to New York after he left the Metropolitan Theater at Forty-Seventh Street and South Parkway in Chicago. When Eubie lived in New York, if he had something musically hard to play he would call Sammy to come over. "Get him a fifth of Old Granddad and set it on the piano," his wife would say. Eubie would do that and then hand Sammy some difficult music. And no matter what it was, classical or not, he would play it on sight. His drinking, however, finally got the best of him.

Many composers, even good ones, do not themselves play the piano. Because of this, they will write nearly impossible sections into their music. The musical "Rhapsody in Black" was written by just such a composer, Ken Macomber. Produced by Lew Leslie, it was a wonderful show, starring such talented people as Valadia Snow and Ethel Waters. Leonard Smith conducted the show and also played the piano. But he was, strange as it may sound, a Bromo Seltzer addict, and one night the habit came on him while he was in the orchestra pit and he passed out. There it was—the show was going on and the conductor stretched out on the floor!

The tenor player, a man called Black Bobby, got out of the pit and went over to Leslie who by this time had panicked. "Lew," said Bobby, "there's a fellow sitting in a box in the theater here who can do it. He can play it," referring to the next big number coming up, Macomber's "impossible" piano piece. Bobby was talking about Joe Steel, a musician like Sammy Stewart. Says Eubie, "He could play the dictionary if you set it up in front of him." "You're crazy," said Lew. "Trust my judgment," answered Bobby. And since Lew had no choice, he did. So Bobby got Joe Steel down into the pit. "Get me somebody to turn the pages for me," Joe said. And he played that difficult number just as if he had played it a thousand times before. Unfortunately, although Joe was extremely talented he was also extremely eccentric. For this reason he couldn't keep a steady job.

The only other pianist whom Eubie has known who could play anything on sight was Elliot Carpenter. He could play a score both forward and backward, literally, playing it first from the top to the bottom and then back to the beginning again. He had been a pupil of Leo Orenstein, who was a great pianist and teacher, but his sight-reading talent was something which no-one could have taught him—it just came naturally.

Another great pianist, Huey Wolford, whose fingers were even longer than Eubie's, was raised up with Eubie in Baltimore. In the early 1900's—around 1905—Huey had a habit of walking into a place where there was a piano player and sneering at him. "Get up, get up!" he would say. "You're ruining the people's music. You don't know what you're doing." And unlike most braggarts, Huey really was good. As Eubie says, "He was my greatest competitor [at that time]." Naturally, however, because of his attitude, nobody liked him very much.

At this time both Huey and Eubie were playing in various

white brothels on what was then East Street. One day when they were playing in Cocky Lewis' place, a white man whom they called Cateye Harry came to town. A "strange-looking character," he had one eye with a slit-shaped cat-like pupil. Half of that eyeball was also white, as was the hair on that side of his head.

Cateye had been "riding the rods" on freight trains—riding on the crossed rods underneath the cars—and of course he was dirty, disheveled and very cold. Walking up to the bar where they served free lunches with their beer, he began to eat the food *without* buying a beer. He was immediately spotted by the bartender. "Hey, what do you think this is?" he demanded. "Don't stop me," said Cateye. "I just got off the rods and I'm hungry." "What can you do?" asked the bartender. "I can play the piano a little bit," answered Cateye. So the bartender told him that before he could eat any more he had to play.

Since Cateye's hands were cold, his playing was pretty poor, but the bartender told him that he could eat anyway. Huey, however, just had to get into it. Walking over to the piano, he looked down on Cateye as if he was dirt until Cateye got up. Then Huey sat down and played for a long time, until his land-lady called him and he had to go out and play for her company. But even though Huey had showed Cateye up, Cateye was still white, and this *was* Maryland, and the white men in the place were not exactly pleased. So Eubie warned the rest of the black musicians not to play anymore until Cateye's hands had warmed up.

Finally Cateye was ready. Sitting down at the piano, he began to play, and he sounded so good that Cocky decided to find out if Cateye could read music, too. Getting a music book out of his office, he gave it to Eubie and asked him to pick out a selection. Eubie picked Liszt's "First Rhapsody" and going to Cateye, he said, "Mr. Lewis asked me to have you to play this."

"Oh yes, sure," said Cateye. And he really played it. Then Eubie picked another one and he played that one, too. Then, turning to the applauding men, he said, "You know, I can play like the colored boys." "I'll stump him," thought Eubie to himself. "I'll tell him to play 'Poet and Peasant' in ragtime." The other musicians had never heard of it, but that ragged-looking hobo played it—just like a black man would.

While he was playing, Huey walked back in. He stood there and listened while Cateye finished "Poet and Peasant" and went on to play some popular songs in ragtime. Walking over to Huey, Eubie said, "I told you you'd run up against your match sooner or later." And for once, Huey had nothing to say.

Cateye stayed around for another two weeks and during that time the other musicians treated him like a king, outfitting him in second-hand—but stylish—clothes, buying him a diamond ring, and taking him "whore-hopping." He was the talk of the neighborhood. Those two weeks were also profitable for Eubie, though, because Cateye taught him some "tricks" on the piano which he was to use later. About Huey, however, Cateye said, "I wouldn't show him nothing." And he never did.

After the incident with Cateye, Huey went uptown and got a job at a white sporting house on Watson Street. Then he played at another white place, the Cascade, on Utah Street, playing with two white musicians, Eddie Claypoole and Eddie Gray. The music never stopped. While Huey was there however, an unfortunate thing happened. According to Eubie, Huey wrote a composition called "Ragging the Scales," and Claypoole and Gray "stole" it from him. They wrote it down and had Harry Van Tilzer publish it, but Huey was never given any credit. "But it was his composition," says Eubie. "I know that."

According to Eubie, the other musicians never liked to play with Huey because he could play in any key. For example, someone might come up and say, "Hey Huey, play Jerome Kern's number." And wherever his hands fell, Huey would play. But the other musicians, playing by music, had to scramble to keep up with him. For this reason he could never get a big band together.

In spite of Huey's conceit and rudeness, though, Eubie has nothing but praise for him. "He was a case all by himself," he says, "a great talent and a great musician. I wish to God there was something recorded by Huey. Then people would know that I'm telling the truth about his ability."

Pianist James P. Johnson was also a friend of Eubie's. Eubie met him in Atlantic City around 1914 when he was playing at the Belmont. Johnson used to come in and relieve Eubie, and he would often ask Eubie to play "that tricky fingers thing" for him. He never played it in front of Eubie; he would just listen to Eubie play it.

Some years later, when Eubie was in New York, he went into Small's Paradise one night and heard the master of ceremonies say, "And now we'll have James P. Johnson play Eubie Blake's 'Tricky Fingers,' " And to Eubie's shock, Johnson played it faster than he himself could!

Johnson's life ended in tragedy, though. He could not leave the bottle alone, even when his liver was so badly damaged that he became delirious, his abdomen swollen like a balloon. Toward the end, Eubie went to see him and tried to persuade him to cut down on his drinking. But it was to no avail. As soon as Eubie left, Johnson managed to get out of his bed and go out and get drunk again. And when he came home that time, it was all over. He never got up again, and he died a short time later.

Still another musician friend of Eubie's was the organist Fats Waller. As a boy he used to play at a theater on One Hundred and Thirty-Fifth Street near Lenox Avenue in New York. "You know, I never liked the pipe organ before that," says Eubie, "but Fats is the guy that made me like a pipe organ." Still in

71

short pants ("Boys wore short pants a long time in those days), he had the most perfect left hand that Eubie had ever heard. Says Eubie, "He never missed. He was perfect."

Many years later Fats, James P. Johnson and Henry Cramer collaborated on a show called "Keep on Shuffling" with Miller and Lyles for New York gambler Arnold Rothstein. (Rothstein was the man reputed to have fixed the crooked 1919 World Series game. He was murdered mysteriously some time after that.) Rothstein had an office on West Fifty-Seventh Street then, but he was out of town and his employees were taking money for themselves instead of paying the musicians. Naturally there was much discontent. One evening Cramer told Eubie that he was going to confront Rothstein and asked Eubie to accompany him. Eubie tried to dissuade him. "Don't do anything you'll be sorry for," he advised. "Maybe Mr. Rothstein don't know about it." But Cramer was adamant, and he went. "Man," says Eubie, "they say Henry turned out the place. He was going to take the roof off!" And although Rothstein wasn't there, Cramer got his money. Whether James P. Johnson or Fats ever got theirs, however, is something that Eubie never found out.

CHAPTER 20

Soon after Eubie went to New York for the next time, he went to work for Baron Wilkins ("The Baron") at the Little Savoy on Thirty-Seventh Street downtown, replacing a pianist named Dude Finley. Dude was a good player and popular with the customers. But he had made so much money that he wanted to go back to his hometown in Florida and show off how successful he was. Baron wouldn't let him leave, though, because he was bringing in the crowds. Finally, in desperation, Dude got someone to send him a telegram from Florida saying that his mother was dying. So even though Baron was suspicious he had to give Dude permission to go. And that was how Eubie got the job.

At this time, Frenchie Waverly, billed as "The Man with a Thousand Songs," was there, as well as a girl—Eubie forgets her name—who would bring the house down with Madison Reed's "Make Me a Pallet on the Floor."

Harry K. Thaw, the millionaire from Pittsburgh, was a regular customer at the Savoy, often bringing in big parties after the theater. One night, however, he came in with a lady, and sitting at his favorite table he ordered a bottle of wine. Just then New York Lovie Joe, a big-time black "sport" and ladies' man, came in, also with a lady. And instead of just a bottle of wine, Lovie Joe ordered a whole basket of wine, making a big show of it. At that, Thaw asked for his bill and left, never to return. He evidently didn't want anybody, especially a black man, showing off his money in front of him.

One night when Eubie was playing, a mean-looking policeman came in, walked up to the piano and prodded Eubie with his nightstick. "I thought I told you to close that piano down and quit playing at one o'clock," he said. Eubie told him that he didn't know what he was talking about. "Don't you get smart with me, boy," shouted the officer, raising his stick. Just then Dude Adams, the floor man, rushed up. "No, no, Mr. Becker, don't do that," he said. "This fellow don't know nothing about your order. He's just been here since the other fellow, Dude Finley, went home." "Well close that _____ music down," Becker said, and walked out, saying something to Baron on the way. When he was gone, Eubie told Baron that he was quitting, but Baron talked him out of it. "I'll take care of you," he promised. "Look at all the money you make here. Besides, that fellow Becker just wanted to act smart. I can take care of him."

But Eubie was never happy there after that. He was living in a tough neighborhood anyway then, on Thirty-Eighth Street between Eighth and Ninth Avenues, and this was the last straw. Soon afterwards he returned to Baltimore.

A year or so later, Eubie picked up a newspaper and there was the headline: "Becker Indicted for Rosenthal Murder." Rushing to his friends, he shouted, "See that guy? That's the policeman who was gonna hit me with that stick in New York!" At first no-one would believe him. Then they insisted that Eubie must have done something. "I didn't do nothing," protested Eubie, "and I wish they'd send him to the electric chair." And that's just what they did. There was a rumor going around for awhile that Becker was never really executed, and someone else went in his place. But Eubie has never believed it. Later, a book was written about the Becker case, casting doubt on his guilt. To Eubie, however, the facts seem obvious. "You see," he explains, "Rosenthal was a big gambler around New York. He was probably slacking up on Becker's pay for his gambling operation, and that's why Becker probably had him knocked off."

Years later, when Eubie was in New York for good and working for Jim Europe, both Baron and his brother Leroy ran clubs in Harlem. "Leroy was a real character," smiles Eubie. "When

74

he got angry, his voice became quite shrill. "You fellows want to fight?" he would squeak, sounding every bit like a "sissy." But as any troublemaker sooned learned to his sorrow, Leroy was not a man to be trifled with. "He'd take him outside and clean 'em."

One night Eubie and Jim Europe were out with Vernon and Irene Castle, taking them on a tour of all of the nice black clubs in Harlem. The Castles wanted to see the dancing. It was an enjoyable evening until they got to Leroy's place and discovered that he wouldn't let them in. Eubie was stunned, because as well as he knew Leroy, he had never before realized that he refused to allow whites into his club. Angry and embarrassed, Jim and Eubie stood outside the door and begged Leroy to let them in. "You know me, Leroy," said Jim. "You know I wouldn't bring anybody in your place that wasn't all right. Why, this is the famous, the great Mr. and Mrs. Vernon Castle." Jim was probably the best-known man in Harlem and his feelings were hurt. "Jim," said Leroy, "I know you, all right, and I respect you. But I don't care who they are. They're white, and they can't come in here. That's my policy, and I'm sticking to it." And he wouldn't let them in.

Years later, when Eubie related the incident to a friend, the man asked, "Why do you suppose Leroy did that?" "I suppose you'll have to dig him up from his grave and ask him," Eubie replied, "because I don't know why." Eubie had met discrimination all of his life and he was used to it, but the Castles had not, and they felt very hurt. On the other hand, when the Cotton Club was the biggest club in Harlem and attracted people from all over the world, the owner, Owney Madden, refused to allow any blacks inside except the help and the entertainers. When Eubie brought his white friends there, even he couldn't get in, in spite of the fact that Madden knew him well. That's how things were back then, and perhaps it was because of this that Wilkins felt that his policy of reverse discrimination was justified.

Baron was finally killed by a man named Yellow Chaleston, a reputed dope addict. "It was a tragic, useless thing," says Eubie. "It shocked everybody in Harlem, because Baron was so well-known and liked by everybody." Yellow had gotten into an argument with two men and needed some money to get out of town, so he went to Baron for a loan. Baron refused, however, not wanting to get involved, and finally in anger Yellow shot and killed him. When the case went to trial, the presiding judge, Judge McIntyre, was an old friend of Baron's. And every time the defense attorneys tried to bring up the issue of temporary insanity, he would always overrule them. "Let's stick to the case at hand," he would say. So Yellow was convicted and sent to the electric chair.

CHAPTER 21

In 1905, soon after the race riot, Eubie moved to New York to stay. In spite of his basic dislike of the place there was work there, and many of his friends were there also.

At that time, many of the "big-time Negroes" in show business lived on Ninety-Ninth Street in Manhattan—where the people to whom Eubie refers as the "swells" lived—including such well-known figures as Ernest Hogan, Cole and Johnson, Bert Williams, and Ada and John Walker. But their work took them uptown to the white theaters, and since racial discord was still rampant that year, they were afraid. So they got Eli Lucas to take care of them.

Lucas was the "baddest" man in New York during that period. A short, light-skinned man, he had served in the black Tenth U.S. Cavalry and was a crack shot. He always carried two pistols, one in each hip pocket. He was so known and feared that if he got into trouble, he would not be arrested. Instead, the police captain would send word to him "requesting" him to come to the station for a "talk." It was understandable, therefore, that with Lucas as their escort the show people had no worries.

Lukie Johnson, the pianist who had worked with Irving Berlin, was in New York, too, then. He was going with a girl named Corrine, a tiny, pretty girl, and he was crazy about her. Unfortunately, when he ran out of money he didn't come to see her. And so finally the inevitable happened. Eli Lucas, who was not only "bad" but also a gambler and a ladies' man, took Corrine away from Lukie.

It was summertime, and in those days Eubie and all of his friends would go to Saratoga for the racing season, where they would play music for the millionaires' parties. "You never saw anything like it," Eubie remembers. "Champagne flowed like water the whole racing season." But when the season ended that year, Lukie returned to New York alone. Corrine had stayed behind in Saratoga with Eli. Lukie didn't know this, however; all he knew was that he couldn't find her. Despondent, he wrote a song about it, called "Has Anybody Seen My Corrine?", and it turned out to be a hit.

When Corrine did leave Saratoga, she still didn't return to New York. Instead, she went to Baltimore to work as a waitress for Tom Smith, the city's chief black politician. He owned a gambling house, run by a man named Kid Pratt, on the corner of Jasper and New Streets, as well as a hotel a block away. A short time later, Eli called Tom to say that he was coming to Baltimore to visit. Tom asked Eli to promise not to go into his place without him. He knew Eli's reputation and didn't want trouble. But Eli disregarded Tom's advice, and on his first day in Baltimore, before seeing Tom, he went into the gambling house to look around.

When Eli came in, a "smart aleck" gambler named Dick Purnell was shooting at the crap table. Eli leaned on the table to watch, and when Dick threw the dice again, they happened to roll up on Eli's overcoat and turned over from eleven to twelve. At that, Dick began to curse at Eli. Eli apologized, but Dick, who always wanted to be thought of as "bad," saw his chance to show off. So he kept on being rude. "Who are you?" he demanded, "I'm a friend of Tom's," said Eli. But Dick wouldn't stop, and when Eli apologized again, Dick hit him. He didn't know who Eli was, of course, but the other men did, and suddenly everyone except the cutter was either under the table or out the door. But Eli didn't do a thing; he just walked out of the gambling house and over to the hotel.

Meanwhile someone had told Corrine about the incident, and she came looking for him. But he didn't want to see her because

78

he knew that she would be angry at him for going into Tom's place. So he started to run, holding onto his pistols to keep them from falling out of his pockets, and Corrine came right behind him. Unfortunately, because he didn't know the town, he was afraid to leave the block. And so there he went, around and around the block, with Corrine still behind him and the men in front of the hotel dying of laughter. "Stop, Eli, stop!" Corrine was hollering. Finally, the last time he ran past the hotel, he gasped, "You all better stop that woman. I'll have to hurt her!" "Yes you might," they laughed, "but she'll drop dead trying to catch you!"

At that time there was a woman gambler in Baltimore named Country Florence who gambled with the men. Every racing season, she would go to Saratoga with Eli and another gambler named Saul Hazelwood, and the three of them would beat the "suckers" out of their money. This year, Eli and Florence had taken a man for three thousand dollars, but when it came time to split up the take with Saul, they tried to short-change him. Unfortunately, the word had already gotten out around town about how much the two of them had "tilted" the man for, so Saul knew that he was being cheated. "No, you're wrong, Saul," protested Eli, but Saul refused to believe him, and they began to argue. At this point, probably fearing what might happen next, Florence walked out and left the men by themselves. Saul was just as bad as Eli—he also carried two guns—and a fight between the two of them could only have one outcome. Finally the men went for a walk, still arguing. "I want my money," Saul insisted. At that, Eli reached for his guns, forgetting that he didn't have them with him. Saul had his, though, and put five bullets into Eli. And that was the end of the bad little gambler. "These days it's hard to believe that such guys really were around," muses Eubie. "What a man!"

CHAPTER 22

Early in his New York days Eubie met Will Marion Cook. Much older than Eubie, he had been born in 1865 in Fredericksburg, Virginia, the son of "free Negroes." He lived to be seventy-nine. After attending Oberlin College, he went to Berlin and studied under Joachim, the world-famous violinist. Later he studied under Dvorak at the National Conservatory of Music in New York, when Harry Burleigh was also a student. He was always seeking to mold the rhythms of black music and ragtime into something new and different. At this time, people like Bert Williams, Ada Walker, George Walker and Ernest Hogan were producing sensational new black shows such as "In Abbysinia," "Under the Bamboo Tree" and "In Dahomey."

Cook wrote an operetta called "Clorindy," which was played at the Casino Roof Garden in New York. It had two great numbers in it, "On Emancipation Day" and "That's How the Cakewalk's Done." Later he formed a group called The American Syncopated Orchestra and he toured Europe with it, making the cakewalk as popular there as it was in this country. His last big work, in the 1930's, was "St. Louis Woman." According to Eubie, however, Cook never got the popular acclaim which he deserved. "He spent his time, maybe too much of it, helping others," he says.

From their first meeting Cook liked Eubie, and he was constantly encouraging him to play better. "Don't be lazy," he would tell him. "Work at your composing. Keep on writing. You learn by doing." When he first heard Eubie's "Charleston Rag," he wanted it published. So the next day they went down to see a music publisher named Kurt Schindler. Schindler listened to Eubie play and then he called his secretary in and told her to make out a check for a hundred dollars, a pre-publication advance. Eubie was elated. But then Schindler looked up and said, "Mr. Blake, I like your piece. But tell me something. Why do you go abruptly from one key to another so much without preparing the listeners' ears?" Eubie was so surprised that he couldn't answer. Debussy was doing the same thing with classical music at this time, but Eubie didn't know it. Years later, Eubie's teacher Rudolph Schramm taught him the Schillinger Method at New York University. The book said, "The ear at first rejects musical innovations which are unfamiliar." But there in Schindler's office, all that Eubie could think of to say was that he didn't know why he wrote that way. Suddenly Cook jumped up and snatched the music from Schindler's hands. "Why don't you respect my protege?" he shouted, and he hustled Eubie out of the office. And although Eubie was embarrassed and disappointed, Cook would not let him take the money.

Cook knew and was known by everybody. He was a close friend and confidante of Victor Herbert, Victor Jacoby and all the leading white musician-composers of those days. And he judged the white performers on their ability and character. He was conscious of everything about them. For example, he didn't care much for George M. Cohan, because Cohan was the only big performer who didn't have a black valet.

Cook had a knack for spotting and recognizing talent. One day he heard Al Jolson singing at Tony Pastor's club on Fourteenth Street, and he thought Jolson was so good that he went to see Lee Schubert about him. "If he's so great," said Schubert, "what's he doing singing down on Fourteenth Street?" "You know, Mr. Schubert," replied Cook, "everybody you see on top of the mountain climbed up there. Nobody jumped up there." But although Schubert said "all right," he never did anything about it. Cook then went to one of Schubert's colleagues and convinced *him* to hear Jolson. This man was so impressed with Jolson's singing that he went back and told Schubert to hire him. Schubert did, putting him on a bill at Hammerstein's Theater for two weeks at seventy-five dollars. But then, somehow or other, he let him get away, and Jolson went into vaudeville.

In spite of his subsequent success, however, Jolson never forgot his friends. Years later, after World War I, when Eubie and Noble Sissle were playing in Providence, Rhode Island, a white man in a "little greasy spoon restaurant" insulted them and ordered them out. Jolson was then playing at a theater down the street, and as they were leaving the restaurant he drove by in his car—a huge Cunningham sedan—and hailed them. When he heard what had just happened he was furious and wanted to go back and "tear up the joint." But although Sissle was all for this idea, Eubie said "No." "If the rabbit bites you once, that's his fault," he said. "But if he does it the second time that's your fault." Some time afterwards, when they were all on Broadway, they would laugh about this incident.

Cook had tremendous influence. He once wrote a white show called "Corrinthia" for George Lederer for Broadway. But the show never got out of the rehearsal stage because of Cook's eccentricity and independence. The show had all white musicians but Cook, as composer, was at the rehearsals, too, of course. One day one of the violinists kept on playing a wrong note. Cook, sitting in the last seat in the balcony of the darkened theater, hollered down for the violinist to repeat the selection. He did, but it was still wrong. "Stop!" yelled Cook. "Right there is where you make your mistake." The violinist couldn't see Cook; he could only hear a voice from the darkness. "Can you do any better?" he asked angrily. "If you can, come down and show me." When Cook went down, though, the musicians saw that he was black, and this upset them. Cook picked up the score and pointed to the passage where the mistake had been made. But the violinist became very rude. "I play for my conductor," he said. "If you can do any better, you show me. Otherwise, shut up!" "Maybe I made a mistake," said Cook meekly. "I'm sorry. But would you please hand me that score?" He took it, tore it into shreds and walked out. Jerome Kern, who was the rehearsal pianist, then re-wrote the whole score and got the credit for it. To this day, Eubie believes that Cook, who had once been in Leipzig, was the one who inspired the eccentric antics of Richard Wagner.

CHAPTER 23

Eubie met his lifetime partner, Noble Sissle, in Baltimore in 1915. Although he had heard of Sissle's reputation as a musician and lyricist, he had never had a chance to meet him before. But one day, while coming from a job in Riverview Park, he met a friend on the stairway leading to the railroad platform. "Eubie," his friend said, "I want you to meet Noble Sissle. He's a grand guy and you ought to know him." They shook hands and made a date to meet the next day. And thus began a partnership of over fifty years. "It was," says Eubie, "a great loving friendship and collaboration."

The first song that Sissle and Blake ever wrote included Eddie Nelson. They took it to Sophie Tucker, who was then appearing in Baltimore at the Maryland Theater, on a Monday, and on Thursday she sang the song. It became a big local success, although Eubie and Noble never got more than three hundred dollars out of it. "Sophie Tucker was a great human being," says Eubie. "She did so many nice things for people, I've got to love her memory."

To demonstrate his point, Eubie recalls an incident with Sophie Tucker which occurred several years later in Philadelphia, where she was playing. Eubie and Sissle were there, too, and they went to her hotel to see her. When they arrived she was still dressing, so her son, who was about eight or nine years old at the time, kept them company. As he talked, he kept calling them by their first names. The men didn't even notice it, but suddenly the bedroom door opened and Sophie flew out in a rage. Slapping her son, she hollered, "They're grown up men, and you've been calling them by their first names. You know better than that, because I've taught you better. Don't you ever let me hear you do that again." Says Eubie, "My goodness, we felt sorry for the child. I hope he don't hate us today for what happened way back then." Reflecting on his love for children and the fact that he, himself, has never had any, he adds, "With all my experience with the other sex I've never even been accused of being a father of nobody's child. Ain't that something?"

After their success with Sophie Tucker they wrote a song for Belle Baker. But she didn't use it. At the time she was married to Lew Leslie. She was appearing at the same place where Sophie Tucker had been, the Maryland Theater, and Eubie and Noble went backstage to see her. But for some unknown reason, her husband made her turn her back to them while they were singing. "Lew Leslie was a little nutty, anyway," says Eubie. "He lost two hundred and fifty thousand dollars [with the International Revue] and commenced to lose his mind with it!" Although Belle told Leslie that she liked the song, he never let her use it. Years later, however, when Eubie was on a U.S.O. tour down at a Southern Army base, he passed Belle Baker in front of the barracks. He hadn't seen her for at least ten years. "Eubie Blake," she shouted, "God love you." And she kissed him. As Eubie puts it, "Eight or ten white guys all dropped dead!"

Eubie's first wife, Avis, used to call Sissle "The Absent-Minded Professor," because he was always forgetting things. But she was actually very fond of him, as is Eubie's present wife, Marion. Sissle's forgetfulness probably stemmed from his World War I battlefield experiences, when he was wounded in France. His recovery entailed major surgery. Then, later, he was seriously injured in an automobile accident and again required surgery. His musical talent, however, was never affected.

CHAPTER 24

As Eubie looks back on his life, he remembers the many acts of kindness from the people he has known. One of these incidents involved a musician named Will Tyler. Eubie was already working with Sissle at that time, writing songs for various white musical shows. The Schuberts would pay four hundred dollars for one; Ziegfield would pay five hundred. On this particular occasion, Lee Schubert wanted a new number to put into his big Broadway extravaganza, "The Winter Garden Revue," and he hired Eubie and Noble to write it for him. Eubie immediately thought of a tune called "Philipino Dance." It had been popular down in Atlantic City and Philadelphia years before, and Eubie thought that it was in the public domain. Nobody had seemed to know where the song had come from. So he "pepped it up" and had Noble write lyrics for it, and they sold it to Schubert for four hundred dollars.

The number was put into the show right away and it was an instant success. A few days later, however, Eubie ran into Will Tyler on the street, and Tyler was furious. "Why did you put my song in the 'Winter Garden Revue'?" he demanded, and he pulled out an old, torn copy of the sheet music, which he had published years before. Eubie was flabbergasted, and he offered to give Tyler his two hundred dollars and put his name on the song. But Tyler was too angry and didn't want any part of it. "Just take the song out right away," he shouted. And Eubie had to agree. First he went to the Winter Garden office and told them to take the song out, and then he went down into the theater. "Vhy you look so sad?" asked the rehearsal pianist in his German accent. When Eubie told him, the pianist looked amused and said, "Vell, you're a composer, aren't you? Can you turn a melody?" When Eubie assured him that he could, the man invited him down to his place in the Village after rehearsal. "I give you my book," he said. "I've got plenty melodies. Take any one you vant." So Eubie went down to his place and got his book of melodies, and he and Sissle wrote a new song for the show. The pianist's name was Sigmund Romberg, and his operettas live on today in the music of America. Says Eubie, "God bless his memory."

CHAPTER 25

"Jim Europe was the biggest influence in my musical career," says Eubie. "He was just something that had to happen in America. He was at a point in time at which all the roots and forces of Negro music merged and gained its widest expression. And he furnished something that was needed in time."

Europe was born in Mobile, Alabama. He reminded Eubie of his father because of his instinct for handling people. "That picture of the great Clef Club Band you see in my house is one of my prized possessions," says Eubie. When the picture was taken the band had just given its first big concert at Carnegie Hall. A smashing success, it opened the door for black musicians and made Jim the darling of the society crowd.

At one time Jim had bands all over the world, and he entrusted Eubie with much of his work, letting him interview, rehearse and hire the black musicians.

Eubie was close to such men as Will Marion Cook, James Weldon and Rosamond Johnson, and Harry Burleigh, the baritone singer and musician. At the mention of Burleigh, Eubie adds, "This young generation of Negroes should know more about him, 'cause he was a great man." At one time he sang as a soloist at St. George's Episcopal Church, the church which J. P. Morgan attended, and later he even sang before the king of England. And when Morgan lay dying, he requested that Burleigh sing at his funeral. In his later years Burleigh worked at Recordies, writing standard arrangements for such well-known spirituals as "Deep River" and "Go Down Moses."

Cook and Burleigh had become friends with Anton Dvorak, the Czechoslovakian composer, at the time when he was teaching at the National Conservatory of Music. Dvorak had a special interest in folk music and he tried to incorporate these melodies into his compositions. At one time he went to live in Iowa for awhile, and during that time he became interested in American Indian songs.

Cook and Burleigh gave Dvorak some black musical themes, and he used these plus his Indian themes in his "New World Symphony." In fact, the second movement, the Largo, is actually the old spiritual "Goin' Home." After this, Dvorak wanted to show his appreciation to his black friends. So he sent Cook and Burleigh to ask Jim Europe to find a place to house a music school. Jim did, through his influence with some white millionaires, and so it happened that for two or three years, until he went home to Europe, the world-famous Anton Dvorak taught music and harmony to little black children in a music school on Thirty-First Street in New York.

Jim was also a good friend and colleague of Hall Johnson. Johnson was from Athens, Georgia. He was highly educated and won many prizes for his musical compositions. In fact, he played the violin in Eubie's Shuffle Along band. He later organized the famous Hall Johnson Choir and then went on to appear in "Green Pastures." After that he went to Hollywood, where he won the Harmon Award for his music in that show.

Jim's brother John was a great musician, too. He was the leader of and pianist in one of Jim's bands, which played at the Copley Plaza in Boston, and he was very popular. Unfortunately John had the habit of going on extended drinking sprees occasionally. And when he did, even Jim couldn't handle him. At those times Jim would call Eubie downtown and say, "You've got to go to Boston right away, Eubie." Eubie would know what had happened, of course, and since he was the only one who knew all of John's piano music by heart, he would go to Boston to fill in for John until he decided to sober up.

John never kept any piano scores to any of his band's numbers. When the publisher sent him any new music, he would play it once and then tear it up. He never explained why he did that. When asked, he would only laugh.

When John was drinking, he would borrow money from everyone. But because of his phenomenal memory, he never forgot what he had borrowed, and he would always pay it back. If anyone tried to claim that he had borrowed more than he actually had, he would quickly set the man straight by reminding him of the exact circumstances of the loan, including what the man had been wearing at the time!

When World War I came Jim and John Noble both went into the Army and became lieutenants. And although Eubie missed them, he was proud of them. "It's hard to explain the stirrings of feelings among Negroes in those far-off days," says Eubie. "It seems they had a natural patriotic feeling. Those were days of a kind of innocence compared with the times we live in now. I guess this was the first time that the knowledge and affairs of the great world affected us in America. Those were some stirring times."

Eubie took Broadway Jones as a partner when Noble left, but he also was in charge of Jim's business and musicians. "I had a swell office," says Eubie. "I had a secretary and everything. It was on the sixteenth floor of this building, and I used to look down on Broadway." Eubie booked all of the top orchestras and musicians, including Billy Tyler, who at the time was married to the present Mrs. Blake. At first blacks weren't allowed to join the musicians' union, but when they began getting more and more work, the officials decided to let them in. The cost, Eubie thinks, was forty dollars apiece.

One day Eubie went down to the union office to pay the dues for some new members. But although the building was open and he could walk down the ground floor hall, he was not allowed into the upstairs office to pay the money. So he went into a phone booth to call them and ask them to let him in.

Just then, however, a group of white musicians who had been arguing loudly in some foreign language began to fight. And in the process Eubie's phone booth was knocked over, glass side down. As Eubie says, "When the bread falls, it always falls on the buttered side." (After that fight, the union split and became two locals instead of one.) The police soon broke up the fight, but Eubie was still trapped. Finally his screams attracted their attention, but since his booth was bolted to four others, it took four men to stand it up again. Eubie had to do a lot of explaining before they would let him go, but they finally did. Says Eubie, "Boy, I have had some crazy experiences in my life."

Jim, meanwhile, organized his famous band of the Three Hundred and Sixty-Ninth Infantry. He was backed by Colonel William Hayward, Daniel Reed and others furnished the group with instruments, and Jim searched the land for the finest musicians he could find. The band was a fantastic success in Europe and was sponsored by the French General Giraud. They traveled all over the continent. And when the war was over, the band paraded down Fifth Avenue in New York as heroes.

Jim then began a concert tour, and, as in Europe, they were acclaimed everywhere. Then, at a concert at Mechanic's Hall in Boston, tragedy struck. In the band was a drummer named Herb. He and his brother had been raised in an orphanage, and perhaps the experience had warped him in some way, because he was always doing crazy things and giving Jim trouble. But Jim kept him anyway.

On this particular night Jim was backstage during intermission talking with tenor singer Harold "Brownie" Browning and Roland Hayes. Suddenly Herb burst into the room, shouting that Jim was always mistreating him and criticizing him. Brownie and Roland left the room so that Jim could straighten out the matter in private. And as soon as they did, Herb pulled out a knife. Jim picked up a chair to put between them, but when he thought that Herb had relaxed, he turned to set the chair down. And when he did, Herb stabbed him in the neck and severed a vein. Fortunately, however, he was rushed to a hospital, where the doctors stopped the bleeding temporarily until surgery could be performed.

Meanwhile a black doctor from Washington, D.C., who had been at the concert rushed to the hospital. "He was," says Eubie, "one of these self-important take-over fellows." Showing his doctor's credentials, he forced his way into the emergency room. "Jim," he cried, "What have they done to you? Are you all right?" "I'm all right," said Jim weakly. "They've saved me." "Le me see, Jim," said the doctor, and before anyone could stop him, he tore off the bandage and re-severed the vein. Jim gave a gasp and he was dead. "It was so useless," says Eubie, saddened by the memory. "It was so idiotic that a great man, Jim Europe, had his life blundered away by two smart alecks. I think of Jim every day of my life."

CHAPTER 26

Like Jim Europe, Eubie, too, had his problems as a band leader. Some of his musicians were "smart alecks." Says Eubie, "It seemed like some of those guys just liked to show off in front of rich white people. I don't know what it was that made them do it. And I can't understand it to this day. But they would show off in spite of everything."

One of those men was a drummer and tenor singer named Wilbur White. He was popular with the millionaires and could therefore help the band make a lot of money. But he was a hopeless show-off.

One night Eubie's band was playing for a big party on Fifth Avenue. The mansion belonged to a millionaire lumber man, and it looked like something out of the movies. A huge curved staircase led to the second floor, and halfway up, on the landing, was a great gilded harp.

Although the hostess had not yet come down from upstairs, the band set up in an alcove off the ballroom and began to play. Things went smoothly for one or two numbers, until Wilbur suddenly ran out of the alcove and up the stairs to where the harp was. He then began trying to play it. Eubie tried to stop him, but it was to no avail. "Aw, you scared of white folks?" taunted Wilbur. "I was born up North." The guests were enjoying themselves, greeting Eubie and complimenting him on his band's music, and Eubie was afraid to argue too much with Wilbur for fear of causing a scene. Suddenly the hostess appeared, dressed like a queen and making her grand entrance. On the landing she touched the harp and then continued down. Coming over to the musicians, she said to Eubie, "You're from Mr. Europe, aren't you?" Then she asked, "Which one of you plays the harp?" The musicians all pointed to Wilbur. "Well," she snapped, "Keep your goddamn black hands off my harp. And all of you get out of here!" Some of her friends persuaded her to allow them to stay, but Wilbur had not yet learned his lesson.

Shortly after the harp incident Eubie's band was hired to play at a birthday party given by a man for his granddaughter. The theme of the party was that everyone was to bring a present wrapped in a five cent red handkerchief. There was a long table in the hall, and as the guests arrived they deposited their handkerchiefs on the table. It was too much for Wilbur to resist. Between numbers, he would sneak over to the table and try to peek inside the presents. Again Eubie tried to stop Wilbur and again he was ignored. Finally, however, it happened. A small white man whom Eubie had noticed at the door walked over next to Wilbur and before Wilbur knew what was happening that man had handcuffed him. Bringing him back to where the band was, he showed Eubie his Pinkerton detective's badge. "I've heard you warn this fellow to stay away from that table," he said. "I could take him downtown right now for attempted theft, but I won't if you'll keep him away from there." He then explained that, by the time all of the guests had arrived, there could be as much as thirty thousand dollars worth of jewelry on the table. Letting Wilbur go, he said to him, "And you'd better pray to God that nothing comes up missing!"

Another show-off in one of Eubie's bands was a comedian named Carl Cook. "I really think Carl was a little bit batty," Eubie says. One day the band was hired to play for a millionaire's bachelor tour. They were to board the yacht in Atlantic City and cruise up to Maine. There were twenty musicians going along, including Jim Europe, Noble Sissle and Eubie, and it promised to be an enjoyable job.

On the train to Atlantic City, however, it was discovered that Carl Cook had stowed away on board. He pleaded so hard with Jim that Jim allowed him to stay, in spite of the protests of the other musicians. They knew Cook's reputation for causing trouble.

The yacht was like a dream, and the band soon got settled and began to play. When Carl Cook's number came up he played his little organ and then began to imitate Bert Williams. The audience was really enjoying the act when suddenly, midway through his shuffling and singing, he reached over, pulled an expensive panama hat off one of the men's heads, and put it on his own head. He then finished his routine, ending it by replacing the hat. The crowd was silent and the hat's owner, without a word, removed his hat and threw it into the water. After an awkward moment everyone applauded, and the man who had thrown away his hat even gave Cook some money. But someone went down below and told Jim Europe about the incident, and although he eventually forgave Cook, Jim was furious. "But that's the kind of experience you had with some musicians," explains Eubie.

CHAPTER 27

Eubie's and Sissle's first Broadway show, "Shuffle Along," came about through a chance meeting in New York one day in 1921 with two musician friends named Miller and Lyles. "Hi," Miller said, "Where you been? I ain't seen you boys since we played over there in Philadelphia." He then went on to tell them that he and Lyles were planning to put on a show, and he thought that Eubie and Sissle would be the perfect ones to write the music. They had heard them do their act and knew that they could write the kind of music Broadway demanded. "We had been playing in the millionaires' homes," Eubie explains, "so I could write like they wrote in those days. Not that I wrote any better, but it was Broadway." Eubie and Sissle agreed to do it. So each of the four men put up one dollar and fifty cents, and they got Al Mayer, a former agent for a big producer, to be their manager. Giving Mayer their six dollars, they sent him over to the McAlpin Hotel to talk Harry Cort, whose father owned a nationwide chain of theaters, into helping them. Harry agreed, but there was only one thing wrong. He, too, was broke. "How you gonna put on a show and ain't got no money?" Eubie asked. "Listen," said Sissle, "These guys can put on a show with a shoe-string. They'll find some way to put it on." And fantastic as it sounds, they really did.

The first thing they did was to go to Eddie Leonard, who had produced the show "Rolly Bolly Eyes," and Frank Fay, who had produced "Frank Fay's Fables." Both shows had been flops, and the two men now offered Eubie and Sissle their old costumes. They accepted them and then, in a totally unprecedented move, they proceeded to write the music to fit the costumes! Eubie's song "Bandana Days," for example, was written to fit the costumes used in the "Rolly Bolly Eyes" plantation number. And from Leonard's costumes they wrote a song called "Uncle Tom and Old Black Joe." They also had to have a parade number, for which they used some tall, beautiful singing girls. They wrote "If You've Never Been Vampèd by a Brown Skin" for these girls.

When the show was written, they rented a society hall on One Hundred and Thirty-Eighth Street between Seventh and Eighth Avenues for rehearsals. A man named Garstoffer kept hanging around and Sissle, who was a moralist, wanted to kick him out. Al Mayer objected, though. "No," he said. "You might need that guy sometime." And he was right.

When rehearsals were finished, they were ready to go on the road. The show was scheduled to open in Trenton, New Jersey, but when they got to the station, no-one had enough money for the train tickets. Eubie was ready to give up and go home, but Sissle still had faith. He could see Mayer a short distance away talking to Garstoffer and he knew that something was up. And sure enough, after awhile Mayer came over and announced, to everyone's relief, that Garstoffer was going to pay for their tickets. And so they got to Trenton after all, and they opened their show that night.

They played in five or six towns in New Jersey, staying two or three nights in each town. And the night they played in Burlington, they knew they had a hit.

Their next stop was to be Washington, D.C. Once more, however, they found themselves short of money. Al Mayer was pacing up and down the platform at the station, wondering what to do, when he met another white man also walking up and down. The man walked up to Mayer and asked, "Did you see that nigger show last night? Wasn't that the greatest thing you ever saw in your life?" "You know," said Mayer, "I own that show." And then he added, "We haven't got the money to get to Washington," and he showed the man his credentials. "Wait a minute," said the man, "I'll send you to Washington." And strange as it may seem, he actually got tickets for all of the seventy-eight people in the show.

They played in Washington for a week and made eight hundred dollars. But one of the theater owners took the money to the race track and lost it. So once again the cast was broke. Their luck was still with them, however, because Mr. Buyers, the theater manager, was a good friend of Sissle's. Seeing their predicament, he gave them the money to get back to New York.

They rehearsed for a week in the Sixty-Third Street Music Hall before they put on the show. During that time critic Allan Dale came to see them, and the next morning he wrote, "It was a night's pleasant entertainment, and the funniest show I've ever seen. But it's a freak show. The music is good, the lyrics good, but I don't think New York will fall for it." (By the term "freak show," he was referring to the bedraggled-looking costumes.) Fortunately, he was wrong. The show was a hit, although when summer came attendance fell off somewhat because of the heat. They put on midnight shows, too, getting all of the show people to come. On some nights Al Jolson brought as many as twenty people. And they charged two dollars and fifty cents per person.

Sissle, who was a good businessman, had begun to worry about other people stealing their material. "Where's the book?" he kept asking Miller, referring to the written copy of the show. "We gotta copyright the book." After much stalling, Miller finally admitted that there was none. He and Lyles just had everything memorized. So they hired four stenographers, two for each side of the theater. And every night for two weeks they sat in the boxes and took down the entire show in shorthand. When it was transcribed, Sissle finally had his book.

One day one of the singers in the show, a man named Hahn, who played the part of Keen Eyes the detective, had to go out of town for a funeral. A replacement, someone who could sing bass, was needed. Several people were considered, including a man named Struck Payne. But Eubie decided on Paul Robeson, who at the time was singing upstairs over a bar at One Hundred and Thirty-Eighth Street and Seventh Avenue. Sissle, Miller and Lyles were unimpressed, but Eubie insisted, even though Robeson had never before been in a show.

Robeson was highly educated and could read music—a natural for the bass part. However, since he had never done a show before, he was unfamiliar with spotlights. The one in this particular theater was in the balcony, and it was especially bright. "Paul," said Eubie, "whatever you do, when you walk out there, don't look in that spotlight." He explained that the bright light would completely blind him. But that night when Paul walked out onto the stage he forgot about the spotlight and looked directly at it. Immediately, he fell into the footlights. He got right up, however, with the band playing to cover him, and began to sing. He was a sensation, of course, and it marked the beginning of his great career.

The show remained in New York for eighteen months, and then they went to Boston to the Selwyn Theater. It was only supposed to be a short run because the great tragedians Faversham and Marlowe were scheduled to follow them. But "Shuffle Along" was such a success that the show was kept at the Selwyn for four months. Finally, however, Faversham threatened to sue the Selwyn brothers, and so the show had to leave.

Their next engagement was at the Olympic Theater in Chicago. A woman named Erlanger owned it, and when Al Mayer called her to book his show, she told him that the only show she wanted was "Shuffle Along," which she had seen in New York. To her surprise and delight, this was the very show which Al had called to book.

They stayed in Chicago for four months, which was a long time, and then they went to St. Louis for two weeks. While there, if they ate in the theater they had to wait until all of the white people had eaten, and even then they were put in the back with screens around them. But that's the way things were sometimes back then, especially in states like Missouri, and so they didn't complain.

Their next stop was Louisville, Kentucky. Eubie had never been down South before in his whole life, and he was terrified. So although it cost him ten dollars a day, he took taxicabs to and from the theater in order to avoid any trouble on the street. They stayed there two weeks, and that was as far South as they went.

Soon they had three shows, with over a hundred people working for them, among whom were Adelaide Hall, Josephine Baker and Florence Mills. Finally, after all this time, they could afford new costumes. The show was now not only marvelous, it was beautiful. At last a show produced by and for blacks had made it on Broadway.

CHAPTER 28

After their success with "Shuffle Along," Eubie and Sissle went to Europe with their wives. During that time, C. P. Cochrane, the producer, was putting on a revue in London, but it was a flop. He had brought in quite a few writers to fix the show up, but they couldn't do it. So when Eubie and Sissle arrived he hired them as his last resort, offering them five hundred dollars per song. And sure enough, they wrote two hit songs, "Taihiti" and "Let's Get Married Right Away," and saved the show. They also wrote "You Were Meant for Me"—a different song from the later one by the same name—especially for Gertrude Lawrence and Noel Coward. It was the first they sang together. In Eubie's home hangs a picture of the revue.

Eubie and Sissle stayed in Europe for nine months. In London they played at such places as the Alhambra Theater, the Coliseum and the Hoban Empire Theater. Beatrice Lillie, a young girl then, appeared on the bill with them at the Alhambra several times. "Oh my, she was funny," smiles Eubie. "She was great even then."

"Cochrane and a man named Kurt Sherman were the finest white gentlemen that I have ever come in contact with to do business with," says Eubie. "[Cochrane] was easily the best producer in the world at that time. The fellow who put on the Follies Bergere in Paris and Flo Ziegfield both used to go over there and go to see C. P. Cochrane's shows and get ideas."

From London, they went to Liverpool, and then Scotland and Ireland, and they played in all of the big cities in the British Isles. But although they went to Paris for four or five days, they never played there.

Now their circuit was ended, and Eubie wanted to go home. This caused the only argument that Eubie and Sissle ever had,

101

because Sissle wanted to stay. They had been a great hit where-ever they had played, and Sissle said, "I'm going down and sign up to do the circuit again." But Eubie put his foot down. "No," he said," I'm going home because I don't like Europe. I don't see any colored people hardly." And he told Sissle that if he did sign up to do the circuit again, he would be doing it alone. So they returned to the United States.

CHAPTER 29

Back home, Eubie and Sissle began a long vaudeville tour on the Keith Circuit, playing all over the country. Although they were paid six hundred dollars per week, they should have gotten more. But they were black, and in those days, black actors and writers were still victimized by the system.

One of the ways in which black song writers were victimized was when they sold a song. The average song publisher would pay two hundred dollars per writer plus royalties, which seemed fair. But then Eubie and Sissle found out that white writers were not only making three hundred plus royalties but were also kept on regular schedules of one hundred to one hundred and twenty-five dollars per week.

When Eubie and Sissle discovered this, they decided to do something about it. At the time they were writing for a publishing firm on Broadway which was run by three brothers. Calling them, they made an appointment for a discussion of new contract terms.

When they arrived for their appointment, the brothers' black chauffeur was standing outside. "I want to tell you boys something before you go up there," he said. "Them guys are waiting for you. They've got it all doped out. I heard them talking." Then he told them that each brother was going to play a role. One would ask questions, one would argue, and one would remain silent. "That way," said the chauffeur, "they figure they got you fellows covered." Eubie and Sissle thanked him and went on up to the office.

Everything happened just as the chauffeur had said it would, and it was so much like a comedy routine that it was all that Eubie and Sissle could do to keep from laughing out loud. Finally, however, Sissle got angry and they both got up to leave. "Wait a minute, boys," said the brothers. "Don't go away mad. We like your music." "Then why don't you pay us like you pay the white boys?" demanded Sissle. And so the brothers acquiesced, giving them not only a raise but a small salary also. It still wasn't up to the white writers' standards, but at least it was something.

Bill "Bojangles" Robinson had traveled all over the country before Eubie and Sissle, so he gave them advice on where to eat and sleep on their vaudeville tour. "Bojangles, God bless him," says Eubie, "was like a travel agency for us." This was important, because in those days, even when a black performer played in the finest theater in town he was usually forced to eat in the "greasy spoons" and sleep in a dump unless he knew of a black family with whom he could stay.

One of their pleasantest experiences on the tour occurred in Des Moines, Iowa. Bojangles' first wife was a childhood friend of Mrs. Lula Macree, whose husband was Des Moines' leading black druggist. And so when Eubie and Sissle arrived in town, Mrs. Macree offered them not only lovely accommodations but excellent food, too. She had a little girl who was, as Eubie says, "a near musical genius," and he and Sissle could hardly wait to get back from the theater each night to play and sing with her.

A few years ago Eubie spoke with Mrs. Macree over the telephone. She remembered him after all that time and told him that her son had graduated from Harvard Law School and was now a judge on the bench of the U.S. District Court of Appeals in Ohio. "It makes me wonder," says Eubie, "about some of these people who say that my race hasn't made any progress."

"We played everywhere and with everybody," Eubie recalls. One week for example, they appeared at the Bushwick Theater in Brooklyn with Georgie Jessel. "Boy, it was fun to be on a bill with that fellow," he says. "He kept you in stitches on stage and off." Another time, they appeared with Ted Lewis.

104

During that time they wrote a white musical for John J. Scholl called "Elsie." They couldn't be in it, of course, since in those days the shows were segregated, but it was a good show and enjoyed a modest success. Scholl wanted to try it out on the road, though, before bringing it to New York.

Eubie and Sissle were appearing at the Olympic Theater in Chicago when they received a frantic call from "Elsie" 's producer. The show was now in Indianapolis, and it was about to fall flat. Could they come and do something to help? What could they say? Even though they weren't in it, it was still their show. So they left Chicago for Indianapolis. When they arrived, however, they found out that the trouble wasn't with the numbers but with the performers. There had been some kind of an altercation and the leading man had walked out on the show.

There was a young handsome chorus boy who knew the part, so they decided to try him out at rehearsal. "What do you fellows think?" asked the producer. "We think he's all right," they said. "He's good looking. He can dance. The only thing is he don't sing too good. But the orchestra can be made to cover for him and carry him over the rough spots. He'll make it all right." And he did. His Broadway debut with the show was a big success, and he later went on to become an important Broadway producer.

Later, around 1930, Eubie wrote a Broadway show with Andy Razaf, who was a fine musician and lyricist. They also wrote many floor shows together. Proud of his race, Andy claimed descent from an African king in the days before black pride became "fashionable."

During that time, Razaf wrote a poem for a Lew Leslie show on which he and Eubie were working. It was called "We Were There," and told of black contributions in all of America's wars, beginning with the death of Crispus Attucks at the outbreak of the Revolutionary War. "It was a wonderful tribute to black heroes," recalls Eubie, who set it to music and took it to Leslie. Leslie listened while Eubie played and Andy sang. When they were finished, he sat in silence for a minute, obviously stirred. But then he looked at them and shook his head. "It's great," he said, "but how am I going to charge ten or twelve bucks for white people to hear this stuff?" Enraged, Andy snatched the music away from him, shouting, "I'll give you my fifteen hundred dollars back!" "Keep cool, keep cool," said Lew, jumping up. "I didn't say I wasn't going to use the material." And he somehow managed to calm Andy down. But he never did use the song.

The only entertainer Eubie and Sissle ever worked with who made it to the top and then snubbed them was Harry Richmond. Whenever he came to New York he would come to the club where Eubie and Sissle were playing, and they would let him sing. He would inevitably be accompanied by a woman to whom Eubie refers as "a beautiful important lady from Hollywood," who seemed to be crazy about Richmond. So when the crowd threw money to him, out of respect for him and the lady, Eubie and Sissle refused to allow him to bend down and pick it up himself. It would demean his dignity, they thought. Years later, after Richmond had become a Broadway star, Eubie saw him one day on Forty-Third Street sitting in a one-seated Rolls Royce and reading a newspaper. Poking his head into the car, Eubie said, "Hi, Harry," but to his shock, Richmond pretended not to know him. So upsetting was this to Eubie that he never told anyone except Sissle about the incident. "He's the only white guy who ever did that to me," he says.

CHAPTER 30

Years later when Eubie and Sissle were starring in a white show produced by Franchon and Marco in Los Angeles, Andy Razaf was there, extremely ill. One day Eubie went out to see him at his mother's house, and it was there that he met Marion, his present wife.

Although their relationship later proved to be a happy one, it was bound to cause trouble, because Marion, being exceptionally light-skinned, appeared white. The fact that she was very pretty made it worse. As Eubie says, "I always had my knife open, all the time."

At the time that he met her, Eubie only had five days to spend in Los Angeles. In fact, their first meeting only lasted ten or fifteen minutes. But when he left he asked her if he could write to her while he was on the road, and she said that he could.

Eubie was only appearing in California then, playing in such cities as Sacramento and San Francisco. And wherever he went, he wrote to Marion every night, being sure to use the dictionary. He had already decided that he wanted to marry her, and he didn't want her to look down on his poor writing.

Finally Eubie was on his way back to New York, but he continued to write to Marion, eventually proposing through the mail. She was hesitant at first, asking him a lot of different questions to find out what kind of man he was. She also had a good job as a secretary for the United States Government, and she didn't want to leave California. But Eubie kept begging her to take a leave of absence and come to New York, and she finally agreed.

Eubie had to go to Memphis next, and he convinced her to go along with him. But because she looked so much like a white woman, it wasn't very pleasant for her. One night two policemen in a patrol car began following them as they were on their way to a restaurant. They followed them for several blocks, talking and pointing at them. Eventually, however, they evidently decided that Marion must be black, for no black man would be foolish enough to be down there with a "sure nuff" white woman, and they took off. Eubie, however, was upset, because he and Marion were not yet married, so that very night he put her back on the train for New York.

When Eubie returned to New York and learned that he had to go to Norfolk, Virginia, he decided that it was time for them to be married. So when they got to Norfolk, they took their blood tests and went to apply for their marriage license. The date was December 27, 1946.

The clerk in charge was a young white man in his early thirties. After asking Eubie the regular questions, he looked around the room and asked, "Where's the bride-to-be?" There were five or six white couples waiting to get licenses, too, and Marion was standing in the back with them. The young man looked at her and then at Eubie. "Is that a white woman?" he asked. "No, that ain't no white woman," said Eubie. "Do you think I'm dumb enough to bring a white woman down here in Virginia to marry?" The man thought for a moment and then relaxed and asked Marion the regular questions, too, and filled out the license. When it was over, however, Eubie hurried into a taxi and then made the driver take a zig-zag route back to their hotel. He was still afraid of the South and didn't want any trouble.

Later Eubie joined a U.S.O. tour in the South, taking Marion with him. He had gotten his first U.S.O. job in 1941 through Sissle. Although Sissle was on the U.S.O. Board, there were no black entertainers. When Sissle found this out, he was incensed and placed a call to Abe Lastfogel, a former agent of theirs, in Los Angeles. "I see you don't have any colored people on the U.S.O.," he said. "Sissle," protested Abe, "don't hold me for it.

They don't want no Negroes in there." "All right," Sissle said, "you get some Negroes on there. And if you don't, I'm gonna tell Walter White [of the NAACP]." At that time, everyone up North was afraid of being exposed as a racist by the NAACP, so Lastfogel said, "I'll tell you what you do. They're having a convention in Chicago and I'll be making a speech, and I'll get you a seat down front. I'll say, 'Look, why there's Noble Sissle.' " At that point, Lastfogel said that Sissle was to get up and make a speech about the discrimination on the U.S.O. tours. So they went to the convention, and Sissle made his speech and got the black entertainers into the U.S.O.

The trains were segregated down South, of course, and every time Marion came up, the same trouble started. The last coach was always reserved for black people. The ticket-collector would collect the tickets outside the train, and when he would get to Marion, he would always stop short in surprise. "You don't go on this coach, he would say. And Eubie would say, "Oh yes she does. This is my wife." "I know, but she's white," would be the reply. "She's not white; she's colored," Eubie would tell the man. "Her mother and father is black." Eventually the man would be convinced, but it was always an unnerving experience. Finally the show got a new manager, a black man named Poke Jones, and he was so afraid of trouble that he refused to let Marion go along. He said that he didn't want to jeopardize his job. This was ironic because he himself, light-skinned and with straight hair, used to have the same problems. But Eubie had no choice. He had to leave Marion up North.

CHAPTER 31

That marriage has been a happy and successful journey into the unknowable country of human relationships. There is the element of loving kindness, a marriage partnership which in this case has lasted beyond the first passionate attraction. And its example produces an unusual example for all those who experience the pleasures of their company. At home, Eubie is a perfect host. His manners have the polish and effortless mark of the perfect gentleman. Away from home, he is the same at all times. Once in Detroit, he was having breakfast downtown with his host for the visit, Freddy Guinyard. Suddenly, he politely excused himself and rose to go out to the news counter for a *New York Times*. A member of the party remarked, "He's a typical New Yorker; must have his morning newspaper." "Yes", replied Freddy, "and let's hope he doesn't meet someone, perhaps a lady he knows. If so, with his elaborate courtesies, he'll be gone a good half-hour". Later that evening, at Freddy's home, Eubie came down stairs in a marvelously chic housecoat. As he made his way carefully, but statuesquely into the room, someone complimented his coat. "Yeah, this coat is nice, ain't it?", he remarked. "My wife Marian bought it for me. She's got swell taste. She buys all my clothing". His evening snack was set before him by Mike, Mrs. Guinyard. As always, he ate delicately, even sparingly of the contents of the tray. He then enjoyed his ever-present cigarette, which is, he mused with a genial nod, "one of the last bad habits I can now enjoy".

Eubie is a serene, happy, and uncomplicated man. He is what the world would consider a successful man who has lived long, accomplished much, and reaped rewards. The world venerates him. He is highly beloved in Toronto especially among members of the Toronto Ragtime Society which has members all over

Canada and in parts of the U. S. The Broadway show "Eubie" is a smash hit. It is built around tunes written by Eubie and has received rave reviews. No greater tribute could be paid a man than the public tribute he was given on June 18, 1978 by President Carter on the White House lawn celebrating the 25th year of the Newport Jazz Festival. Eubie appeared and stole the show. He is acclaimed on several continents. He is past the stage where fame turns his head. He is truly one of America's treasures.

INDEX

INDEX

INDEX

INDEX

The author, Lawrence Taylor Carter, is a native of Iowa who has resided in Detroit for more than 50 years. He was educated in Iowa and Michigan. He studied drawing and painting at the Wicker School and the Detroit Society of Arts and Crafts, and harmony composition at the Detroit Conservatory of Music. He has contributed columns to the *Michigan Chronicle* and the former *Detroit Independent*. For several years, he conducted a radio talk show called "black viewpoint" over Detroit's WGPR. He has written book reviews for the *Pittsburgh Courier*, commentaries on ragtime and jazz for the *Detroit News*, and has published short stories for literary quarterlies. Since 1969 he has written a regular weekly free lance column for the *Detroit News*.